What to Tell, Whom to Tell It, And When to Tell It

Here at last is a substantial alternative to the indiscriminate self-disclosure encouraged by today's 12-step programs, psychotherapists, and an exploitative media. This affirmative book, written by two experts in the therapeutic movement, teaches you how to differentiate between inappropriate revelation and wisely considered confessions that will lead you to new plateaus of emotional and spiritual maturity. You'll find compassionate and enlightening discussions of:

- Generational secrets and myths that bind—and blind—families through the years
- Sexual secrets that affect current relationships
- "Dark" secrets we keep even from ourselves, covering old hurts, pains, rages, angers, and grief.

Secrets to Tell, Secrets to Keep

SECRETS TO TELL, SECRETS TO KEEP

Terry Hunt, Ed.D. and, Karen Paine-Gernée

ISBN: 0-965-6788-1-4

Cover photo by: Daniel Bianchetta
Cover design by Arana (arana@cavedrawings.com)

Havenhurst Press
214 Market Street
Brighton, MA 02135

Terry Hunt can be reached at:
Market Street Health
214 Market Street
Brighton, MA 02135
(617) 787 - 3511 • fax - (617) 787 - 5045
e-mail: Thunt02138@aol.com

We dedicate this book to all those searching for the personal meaning of the secrets of their lives without giving up respect for their own and others' modesty, humility and privacy.

Contents

PREFACE TO THE NEW EDITION

Much has happened on the world stage and on television talk shows since this book was published that magnifies the need for individuals to clarify their relationship to information about themselves and others. Confidentiality is no longer a given if enough pressure put to bare, even among friends. The idea that people are entitled to know if they are the least bit curious seems to carry the day. The claim of privacy means that you have something sordid to hide. Finally, few holders of secrets consider where and when is the right time or place to unburden themselves.

Karen's death continues to inspire me. It is amazing to me that the secret benefit of "good" grieving is lost on so many who would prefer to just get through it. Grieving well leads to a state of grace where the departed individual lives on deeply embedded in the griever's heart. She truly cared about the preciousness of each individual's life. To live an authentic life is to have a precious private inner world.

It was this shared concern that lead us to write a book about protecting yourself and others from the damaging effect of improper management of secrets. Telling "all" to anyone you are intimate with continues to be a very high-risk and often unkind and uncivil way of living. Withholding information for the sake of conflict and pain avoidance is just as unkind, even if it keeps the peace. The core purpose of this book remains critical: we need to learn and practice the skills of sharing difficult information and feedback with others constructively.

Creating intimacy with oneself is so important in this age where best friends move away and neighbors only know your name. With e-mail and phone service growing more and more universally available and affordable, it is possible to maintain contact across the world. It is in this new world that guidelines for verbal intimacy become more and more important due to the absence of physical cues like eye contact and touch. I am so pleased that we are able to republish these useful tools.

Terry Hunt
January 1999

Acknowledgments

It is very hard to write complete acknowledgments when one of the authors die before the book is published. Karen succumbed to cancer on April 25, 1993, but her inspiration lives on in every page of the book.

Larry Rothstein, Ed.D., took us through the many rewrites of the project and has been a delightful companion and support every step of the way. Jamie Raab's encouragement on the publishing side could always be counted on. Kris Dahl stewarded the project through its conception and acceptance. New ideas need the faith of people like these if they are to receive a larger audience. We are very grateful.

A number of other friends took the time to read the manuscript during its production and each gave valuable feedback; Diane Marks, Joanie Bronfman, George Whiteside, Richard Perl and Rick Paine. Eileen Power and Moching Yip have kept the manuscript moving forward through every rewrite and computer glitch. My wife, Gale, and three sons, Evan, Avery, and Oliver, have put up with deadlines and periods of personal struggle as I carried on after Karen died. Karen's husband, Rick, lived a hero's life as he helped Karen write when she felt up to it and let go of the project when she became too sick. Karen's children—Alex, Megan and Max—were steadfast in their presence through it all.

There are many others who have contributed their loving support as well as their secrets. We have used these secrets to illustrate our thoughts. We thank them all. While all the stories are substantially accurate, many details have been changed to protect the anonymity of those who shared their stories with us on their healing journeys. Please use these stories in the same spirit. They are precious gifts that can inspire, sometimes to be told, sometimes to be kept to one's self. The fundamental purpose of this book is to help you know the difference.

Finally, we are very interested in your response to those ideas and would love to hear from you. Or if you would like further information on our previous book and video, both entitled *Emotional Healing,* or on workshop schedules and locations, write to:

Market Street Health
214 Market Street
Brighton, MA 02135

—Terry Hunt, Ed.D.
June 1994

Introduction

In our first book, *Emotional Healing*, we disclosed a great deal about ourselves. It was cathartic for us to put in print the truths of our lives. Using our own experiences and our clients' stories, we argued that individuals who grow up in alcoholic and abusive homes learn a profoundly incorrect method of living— pain avoidance. As children we ignored the pain, substituting power and control for healthy pleasures and personal fulfillment.

We believe pain-avoidant behavior ends when you reexperience directly childhood pain, rage, and fear. As an adult, you are able to bear such childhood feelings without blame or recrimination. Once done, you can reclaim your capacity to lead a satisfying life. Emotional sobriety comes from the hard work of telling ourselves and others the truth.

We did this emotional work in private settings, however—what we call "sacred space," far away from the curious and sometimes judgmental scrutiny of the public. Our friends and lovers did not witness our healing. Although we applaud the explosion of twelve-step fellow-ships and other self-help programs, we believe that privacy is being lost and is being replaced with a new standard of "therapeutic friendship" and "if you love me, you will tell me all." This book is about our sense that our culture has gone too far with self-disclosure and is "psychologizing" our every thought and action.

The healing process needs to remain mysterious, personal, and sacred. Telling secrets in the wrong place to the wrong people dissipates the resolve to become emotionally sober and harms recovery. We've found out the hard way that there are secrets to keep.

Moreover, we believe that life after recovery is centered on relationships between individuals who see each other for the pleasure of their company, not to help each other work out emotional problems. In such relationships, excitement comes from interacting with other healthy people who know the limits of intimate self-disclosure.

This has become true for both of us. We have been best friends for seventeen years. We were drawn together by our shared concerns, some horrendous fights, and many tears. We say that "we can tell each other everything." But these days, we often don't. We have tired of sharing every drama. Instead, we think carefully about the pleasure in our friendship. We separate what enhances our relationship from what is mere gossip or simply information to fill "dead air."

Having a sense of mystery about the other makes it exciting to be in touch and to lead workshops together. Recently, we gave a talk with little planning, and it worked out well. The lecture was spontaneous and interesting for everyone. Keeping our marriages full of the same excitement is *harder,* but *possible.* It involves the same kind of decisions about sharing information with our spouses and maintaining our independence and mystery.

In this book we look at the choices you have about sharing your secrets. We want you to make choices with care for yourself and others. We want self-disclosure to deepen your relationships and strengthen your connection to your soul. In *Secrets to Keep, Secrets to Tell* we offer a number of tools—the Stages and Phases of Emotional Healing, the Life Enhancement Grid, the Body Scan—to help you ask the right questions about secrets and to differentiate the pursuit of pleasure from therapy.

Our views on secrets and the tools we offer have been deeply influenced by Bioenergetic analysis, a school of psychotherapy pioneered by Alexander Lowen, M.D. He and other Bioenergetic therapists view individuals as a mixture of reason and emotion, able to contain and express intense feelings. In Bioenergetic analysis, healing consists of becoming aware of the innate intelligence available through the body and its feelings. We believe this intelligence is far more profound than the normal internal dialogue and other chatter that goes on in our minds.

We also feel that there is a spiritual meaning to human pain and suffering. Life is a set of personal decisions about what we share and what we keep to ourselves. A phrase encapsulates the problem: "The difference between the mystic and a madman is that the mystic knows whom not to talk to." This book helps you find the mystic within yourself.

Dr. Lowen wrote a short paper entitled "In Defense of Modesty" (unpublished essay from an *International Bioenergetic Society Newsletter,* Winter 1991) that bears particular interest. He suggested that the desire for privacy is not founded in shame but rather in a sense of inner sanctum within which one's potency develops. He contrasts the seductive quality of a suggestive bathing suit with the childlike asexual innocence commonly experienced when everyone is disrobed by consent. Thus, it is not what you see but what you are prohibited from seeing that enhances mystery and expresses your potency. In the same way, we regard secrets, both traumatic and delightful, as treasures to be shared with others only by careful decision, and at the right time.

Secrets to Tell, Secrets to Keep assists you on this journey in a logical, step-by-step manner. In chapter 1, "The Problem with Secrets," we explore the razor's edge between the confession that liberates and the indiscriminate self-revelation that harms. Chapter 2 discusses the origins of the voyeuristic society that is undermining true healing. Chapter 3 describes how the therapeutic movement has worked hand in glove with the voyeuristic impulse. Chapters 4 and 5, respectively, introduce two powerful tools—the Stages and Phases of Emotional Healing and the Life Enhancement Grid. The rest of the book looks at the variety of secrets people face: generational (chapter 6), family (chapter 7), sexual (chapter 8), lower self (chapter 9), and higher self (chapter 10).

What makes life exciting? The answer must be tailored to each individual. Not knowing keeps mystery alive, but excessive secretiveness causes repression, paranoia, low self-esteem, and loneliness. How do you find the balance? Through the choices you make. We cannot tell you what they should be, but only how and why to make them. But this we can assure you—there is excitement and pleasure in the discovery of which secrets to tell and which to keep.

The stories that we recount are pulled together from

persons we have met along the way. Their identities are disguised by having changed insignificant facts and by compositing details from various people's lives. The secrets told in this book belong to the people from whom they originate, and we are grateful that their sharing of them has enriched our lives. We hope that these secrets help you find a clear path in dealing with your own.

Special Note from Terry

Within the month that Karen and I completed the first draft of this manuscript, she succumbed to the breast cancer she had been struggling with for seven years. This book is only part of how her teaching goes on, because it is in the hearts and minds of those who knew her. As this book was written by the two of us, I have chosen not to change the verb tense that Karen and I used.

1

The Problem with Secrets

Until a generation ago, society believed that we should keep our secrets to ourselves, or at least behind the front door of the family house. Now, however, a new culture of openness understands the shame and burden that secrets place on us. In therapy and self-help groups we tell our innermost thoughts, confess secret deeds, and admit abuses we have suffered. Such activities free us from depression, anger, and pain, and make energy available for the pursuit of fulfillment and pleasure. The only way out of misery, many have learned, is through it.

Our society was moving in a good direction, toward what we have called emotional healing. But in the past few years the new openness has gone too far. On television talk shows, invited guests reveal deep emotional pain, often with the individual who inflicted the harm seated right next to them. Inevitably, the victim breaks down, the camera zooms in and the host expresses sympathy and concern. This is not healing, but exploitation. Voyeurism has become commercially viable. Moreover, this form of self-disclosure robs people of the personal mystery and privacy crucial in creating individuality and self-esteem.

Where Is the Line?

The question that we all need to ask is, where is the line between the confession that liberates and the indiscriminate self-revelation that harms? Let us look briefly at four situations where this question is pertinent.

Eddie and Siri

The guests in the church cheered when Eddie and Siri got married. Their courtship, a long drawn-out affair filled with dramatic endings and tearful new beginnings, had tried the patience of everyone they knew. As Eddie slid the thick gold band onto Siri's finger, Roanne, his lover of a year, watched. She was happy with dating a number of men, and only occasionally seeing Eddie. Both Eddie and Roanne assumed that their relationship would continue.

However, friends urged Eddie to tell Siri his secret in the name of openness, communication, and intimacy. When he did, Siri exploded in rage and indignation. After months of acrimony, Siri's anger had not subsided and she left Eddie. Stunned, Eddie regretted ever telling her about the affair.

Marti

Marti, an attractive thirty-six-year-old health insurance administrator, was the "strong silent type." Her message to the world was, "I don't need anybody. I am self-sufficient." And on a superficial level she was. But her image masked family secrets that kept her unhappy.

Marti was full of emotion and sexual passion. To keep relationships at a fever's pitch, she would end them after only a few months. What Marti didn't realize was that she didn't have the tools to be intimate, particularly the ability to expose her inner life to a lover. Marti's unresolved conflicts impelled her toward new and fun relationships and away from her secrets.

Celeste and Arthur

Celeste, twenty-seven, an administrative assistant in a small office, was "coming apart at the seams" because of perpetual conflict with her boss, Arthur. They fought continually over little things, such as how to organize her workload, how to respond to clients, and even which coffee service to use.

Rather than finding practical solutions to their problems, Celeste and Arthur "pushed [each other's] buttons" by using psychological tools they had learned in therapeutic environments. This psychologizing of the situation led to explosive confrontations. They both wished they knew far less about the other and that they had not revealed so much.

Tanya and Gary

Tanya and Gary lived lives that most people would envy. They were both forty, financially secure, healthy, and had three thriving children. Yet their marriage was in disarray.

The excitement each felt for the other in the first

eight years of their marriage had evaporated after the children were born. They were constantly tired and irritated, sexually frustrated, and bored with the routine of raising kids. But most profoundly, they grieved for the emotional depth that they had once shared. They needed secrets to create the mystery essential for a happy marriage.

In each case, our clients struggled with the dilemma of which secrets to tell and which to keep. As we worked with them, we encouraged the expression of intense feeling, and nurtured psychological strengths like self-esteem and self-awareness. In contrast to the public exposure of secrets that occurs hourly in the media, this exploration went on in what we call sacred space.

Sacred Space

Sacred space is an arena for the sharing of something precious. It is a place of silence and respect, where no judgment is rendered. In a sacred space, the receiver of the confidence listens with all senses alert, hearing the meaning behind and between the words. The intent of a sacred space is that a secret ought to be revealed in an atmosphere of unconditional love so a person can unburden himself or herself and heal.

Creating a sacred space may be as simple as announcing to a trusted friend that you have something important to tell, or as complex as an elaborate ritual, such as the lighting of candles, reciting "holy" words, sitting in a circle, playing music, or meditating together. Alone in the wilderness, at a therapist's office, in self-help groups, or in the privacy of their own homes, people can create a sacred space for themselves.

We tell our clients that when they share something in a sacred space, they should feel the sharing went somewhere. No longer is it their secret alone. This has a cathartic effect. Emotional healing does not occur every time a secret is shared. It takes practice and careful attention to the task of healing. But eventually, a profound change occurs in a person's life.

Stages and Phases of Emotional Healing

In addition to a sacred space, we introduced our clients to a powerful concept: that there are stages and phases of emotional healing during which they relate to their secrets in very different ways. Many people we see are in the stage we call "stuck in the telling," where individuals have their life run by their secrets and seem to need to talk about them repeatedly. Emotional healing takes time, often requiring revisiting the experience of traumatic secrets again and again. As you progress to later stages of emotional healing, your relationship to your secrets must change, and you must think about a variety of factors before you decide what to tell and what to keep to yourself.

The stages of emotional healing are

- Stage 1—*In the Soup:* In this stage, denial predominates. People live in the "it wasn't so bad" fantasy.
- Stage 2—*Shame Keeps You Silent:* Here people are aware of their secrets but feel so much shame that they don't tell anyone about them.
- Stage 3—*Telling the Secret—Recovery Begins:* Now

telling secrets begins to work. Deep grief and anger are expressed. As people recover, they overflow with emotion.

• Stage 4—*The Telling Works:* As people tell their secrets, energy that was bound up in denial and repression becomes available for playfulness and joy. Small successes lead to rising self-esteem.

• Stage 5—*Stuck in the Telling:* Telling secrets becomes a trap. People become therapy junkies, stuck in self-disclosure. Confession follows confession.

• Stage 6—*Secrets to Tell, Secrets to Keep—Emotional Maturity:* Now people can discriminate between the secrets they need to tell to enhance the quality of their life and those they choose to contain so as to develop a stronger sense of themselves. Here people operate out of free choice.

• Stage 7—*Freedom:* At this stage, people understand who they are and what they want, and accept life's unfolding.

Within each stage, a three-phase process operates:

• *Exploration:* Family history and the unconscious motives for your actions are examined

• *Catharsis:* Feelings of fear, hurt, rage, and grief are expressed

• *Individuation:* An increasing sense of personal responsibility pushes you to the next stage

At the end of this chapter is a summary of the stages and phases of emotional healing. Study it. You will be seeing such charts throughout the chapters on generational, family, sexual, lower-self, and higher-self secrets. (For further explanation of the chart, see chapter 4.)

Finally, we give our clients two powerful tools to help them handle their secrets: The Life Enhancement Grid and the Body Scan. The Life Enhancement Grid is a simple but effective way to make the difficult decisions about when and with whom to share your secrets. The Body Scan enables people to understand the body's language and use it as a trusted consultant. We will describe each of these tools in depth later in the book. But for now, let us look again at the situations we introduced earlier.

Eddie and Siri

Eddie and Roanne's affair might have continued for a long time had Eddie, Siri, and Roanne not been a part of a community interested in holistic health and psychotherapy. The community was committed to opening up childhood secrets, sharing of feelings, and encouraging personal disclosure. In keeping secret his relationship with Roanne, Eddie broke a major tenet of the community.

EDDIE: "The two relationships were separate in my own mind. I think most men can do this, but I felt pressure to change the situation. I just didn't know which way to go. I got into this affair when Siri and I were separated. I didn't feel bad about seeing Roanne. It was the secretiveness that bothered me."

SIRI: "Looking back, I know that I must have sensed betrayal. But then I just thought of it as our having difficulty with transitions. I believed that I needed to feel more connected before I could relax back into the relationship whenever we had been apart. I felt ashamed, however, at the intensity of my withholding. It makes me furious even today to think that I took my coldness as my problem when *my* body told me something was wrong."

After Eddie's revelation, Siri tried to deal with his secret. She valued honesty but found herself wishing that Eddie had stopped sleeping with Roanne and had never mentioned his affair. She gave her feelings of fury and betrayal full voice, believing they would abate. But month after month, the rage continued, even though she saw a therapist regularly. To cope with her anger, Siri went on eating binges, gaining fifty pounds.

Siri and Eddie retreated into "victimized" identities: he, the abused husband; she, the wronged wife. "If only Eddie would acknowledge how deeply he has hurt me," thought Siri, "then we'd be all right." Eddie tried, but nothing satisfied Siri. After several months, when her daughter Caroline finished school, Siri fled with her to Seattle.

Eddie and Siri had been separated for a year when they came to our twelve-day workshop at the Esalen Institute in California. They both wanted to get back together. Over the year they had been in touch by phone and realized how much they cared for each other. Eddie had broken off his relationship with Roanne, and neither he nor Siri had formed any other romantic relationships. At the workshop, Eddie learned he had gone from inappropriate concealment to indiscriminate sharing. He was "stuck in the telling" stage of emotional healing. Eddie did not think carefully about how telling might affect Siri or even understand what he had hoped to accomplish. In fact, Eddie realized at the workshop that his relationship with Roanne had indicated that he longed for more warmth and love from Siri. But a deeper secret prevented him from being aware of this: his sense of manhood and his ability to stand up for himself had been injured by his father's unaffectionate, distant, and critical nature.

Siri, for her part, also found a deep secret. When Siri was a teenager, her mother raged and punished her for sexual activity that had never occurred. Siri knew that this was her mother's own guilt, but Siri was still fearful of her own sexual impulses.

Eventually Eddie and Siri understood that telling the truth brings people closer. But it needs to be done in a sacred space. Eddie and Siri also learned several other things:

- *There is a dramatic difference between privacy and withholding.* Eddie's infidelity was withholding, and Siri unconsciously knew about it. Because she wanted to distance herself from Eddie, Siri blamed herself for her coldness. Withholding can drive someone crazy because he or she will seek explanations without all the facts. It did not enhance Siri's life to wonder if she was paranoid or frigid.

We believe a healthy person is guided by an inner wisdom, or a "soul," that can be heard through the language of the body and its feelings. Healthy individuals are not adverse to correction, however painful, as they pursue fulfillment and pleasure. Healthy people look for mutually satisfying, life-enhancing solutions to conflicts. We will show how this applies to secrets in chapter 5.

- *Important secrets need not be shared.* We agreed with Siri that her privacy was violated by Eddie's disclosure. He could have simply stopped his affair, for infidelity rarely enhances an intimate relationship. When infidelity is life enhancing, extraordinary circumstances exist, and we will address these in chapter 8, "Sexual Secrets." In this case, Eddie needed help objectively sorting out the meaning of his actions. But Siri and Eddie's friends were unable to do this because their own fears were activated by the drama. Eddie really needed time to work through his childhood pain so that he could be strong enough to ask for what he wanted from his marriage to Siri. He caused enormous suffering by "letting it all hang out." The secrets of his unhappiness about this new marriage were hard to share. He felt like a failure, a devastating experience for anyone. By exploring that feeling, however, he saw his affair as a defense against the pain he unconsciously thought he could not bear.

Revealing important secrets, or giving critical feedback without "preparing the ground" for healing, can be harmful in two ways. First, by confronting old wounds without a context, a person can become frustrated, wondering whether healing really can take place. Second, self-disclosure becomes mundane, part of the secular dialogue of a voyeuristic society. People score points by identifying their own or other people's failings. This is cruel. People rarely benefit from having someone else discuss their "issues" over dinner, although it may make for interesting conversation.

Marti

Marti came to us because of our work with Adult Children of Alcoholics (ACOA). When the explosion of interest in this phenomenon occurred, she knew that one of her secrets—her mother's alcoholism—needed to be explored. She had distanced herself from her family, but at this point in her life she was distancing herself from men as well. She was in the "Shame Keeps You Silent" stage.

MARTI: "When Karen talked about her mother's drinking problem with seriousness and compassion for both her mother and herself, I knew I wanted to learn from her. As an adult, I had not thought about my mother's problems, focusing on her love for me. I had no idea I was so deeply affected by my mother's habits. She had rarely embarrassed me in public or had been so drunk that she could not manage the household or her job. Karen helped me see that I was actually very sad and angry about my mother's failures and her inability to be an admirable role model for me. I couldn't admit how sad and angry I really was. I didn't like the person I met inside me.

"Slowly I discovered I was suspicious of all my emotional attachments because of the fracture in that first one with my mother. I wanted to be close, but not too close. I couldn't disagree with someone without terrible anxiety. I kept my most precious secrets to myself, such as my fear that I would lose control with food the way my mother did with alcohol."

Marti was fun to be with as long as you did things her way. Her friends went along because she brought joy and good ideas to every occasion. Only when she developed a deep and intimate relationship with Karen did Marti realize how shallow her other relationships were. Karen would ask questions about painful aspects of her life and not let Marti change the subject. Karen listened and believed Marti, an experience Marti had never trusted fully before. She loved Karen's kindness and presence.

Marti found in Karen a person willing to give Marti the sort of focused attention that she had never experienced before. People usually cannot fully thrive in the world without focused attention, but often we don't know it is missing from our life until we experience it. Focused attention occurs in sacred space, where communication takes on a unique importance for both listener and speaker. Talking about secrets with friends does not provide the same healing because friends usually feel obliged to ameliorate or even fix the pain for us. Karen, instead, provided a context for Marti to feel her grief and longing. If Marti had poured out the pain to a friend or lover, she would have perceived herself, and perhaps would have been perceived, as "needy."

Focused attention is not voyeurism. To show vulnerability is a skill that Marti needed to learn before becoming intimate with someone. Her vitality and joy was a necessary but not sufficient ingredient for having healthy relationships. Long-term relationships require more of a person, as we shall see in chapter 8, on sexual secrets. Sexuality, by its nature, activates the wounds of childhood, but it also offers an adult the intimacy that sustains relationships for a lifetime.

Marti also learned that the healthy person operates according to the principle of harmlessness derived from Buddhism. By "harmlessness" we mean that healthy people find it distasteful to deceive, seduce, or otherwise take advantage of another person while pursuing their own personal pleasure. Marti had never invested herself in her personal relationships because she had not faced her dark side, which we will call the lower self. Only by exploring her lower-self secrets, as we will show in chapter 9, could Marti face life with an open heart and discover her own harmlessness.

Healthy aggression is used not against other people or things, although sometimes it may look that way. Rather, the focus of this kind of aggression is *for* something you care about, always allowing for compromise and pushing for mutually satisfying solutions. Learning this becomes the challenge of living in a world driven by greed, dishonesty, and hate, where aggression is used against others in a destructive way. We explore how these higher-self secrets emerge in chapter 10.

Marti's story has a romantic ending. As her capacity for loving expanded, she contacted a man, Jack, she had broken off with several years before. Her memories of Jack were of his warmth and his ability to negotiate problems without giving up or getting mad. She wanted to be close to Jack now because she was able to feel for him in a way that had not been possible before.

Celeste and Arthur

Arthur, thirty-five, came to see us again after his battles with Celeste had reached a fever's pitch. In the several years since Arthur was our client, his self-esteem had improved and the depression that had plagued him in his twenties had diminished. But he still felt socially inept and sexually frustrated. He was in "The Telling Works" stage.

It was immediately clear that part of Arthur's problem was that he was attracted to Celeste. As her boss, he did not act on his feelings at work and kept his attraction to her secret. But he revealed many other secrets—his abusive parents, their subtle acts of hostility toward him, and his desire to please authority figures.

Celeste, for her part, listened sensitively, drawing on her experience as a volunteer student counselor. Yet, she resented Arthur for talking about these matters at work, which she thought were inappropriate topics. Finally, she exploded at Arthur after he had drawn out of her that she was having boyfriend difficulties, along with money problems (a coping mechanism she had learned from her mother, who resented Celeste's absent but financially successful father).

Arthur's relationship with Celeste had many features of a frustrated love relationship, an idea he angrily rejected at first. Celeste's wanting to "do things her way" had a vehemence to it that seemed to say "you can fire me, but you can't control me." Arthur was caught in the bind of wanting to control her but not lose her.

We emphasized to Arthur that as the person with authority it was his job to take the lead in managing the relationship. After some emotional work, Arthur separated his rage at his mother and father from his concerns about Celeste. He suggested to Celeste that at work they converse only about job-related tasks. He also told her he would respect her prerogative to first try things her own way, saying he would only offer suggestions when solicited.

Things settled down for several months. After further work on his fear of his sexuality, Arthur realized it would be life enhancing for him and Celeste if he admitted his attraction to her. The conversation went well, and Celeste thanked him for his honesty. Over the months, they developed a warm and respectful working relationship.

Arthur and Celeste each had to learn that there were some things to tell, and some things not to share. Healthy modesty is not inhibition or being "uptight," rather, it states to the world: there is something precious inside that I share with a privileged few, in the context of mutual respect, and there are some things about me that I may choose to tell no one.

For those of us who grew up in families where we were not allowed to tell our secrets, not sharing ourselves is firmly ingrained. When we open ourselves up in therapy or in self-help groups, the relief may be so great that secrets fly out of us. We cannot contain them, nor do we want to. For the first time, our sense of isolation is broken down through self-disclosures. This is an important step—but it can become addictive because we can come to need the relief we feel when we get something off our chest.

When you come to an understanding about something in your past and then tell someone about it, you imagine you have control over your life. Just as an alcoholic thinks he or she is helped by a drink, the sense of control makes you feel better for the moment. Oftentimes, however, these self-assurances are limited. As Celeste and Arthur's case demonstrates, you have to live with the consequences of your stories.

Figuring out why Celeste was insistent on doing things her way was really not as important as getting the job done. On the other hand, Arthur's disclosure of his attraction to Celeste enhanced both their lives. The disclosure contained an apology, as well as a compliment to Celeste. In addition, the timing was right, for it cemented the peace they had already worked out.

Tanya and Gary

By the time Tanya and Gary had made their first therapy appointment, their once-happy house had become a war zone. Home was Tanya's domain, and both had tacitly agreed that she "knew best" about domestic matters. Gary felt like the odd-job man, expected to do whatever he was told in return for a bed and access to the refrigerator. Gary resented this but was also ashamed of how he impulsively used sarcasm to respond to the tension.

Both feared the nightmare of separation and divorce, so they tried to work things out. But under stress, they inextricably vented their frustrations on each other. They were both in the "Telling the Secrets—Recovery Begins" stage.

Fears permeated their thoughts: Gary was unsure of himself as a father and a lover. His fear of Tanya's anger shaped his actions. He would lash out at her over petty issues that were excuses for pent-up rage, only to feel contempt for himself and his impotence. Tanya's fears were tied up with a sense of her impotence also. She thought, "Can I stand up for what I want without thinking of myself as a bitch?" She felt lost in the details of life, and dreaded every day.

Even though they both knew better, Tanya and Gary attributed their own personal suffering to others, exhibiting behavior that is a natural defense for wounded individuals. Finding a sacred space to talk seriously about their feelings was the first step. They needed to express their vulnerabilities to each other, but they also needed to learn how to deal with their problems in a constructive way.

Gary and Tanya's marriage required not only more sharing time together but also more fulfilling moments when apart. Specifically, Gary joined a men's group that gave him a sense of male support and friendship. Tanya found a mother's support group that provided similar help. Intimacy with others built up their self-esteem and began the process of re-creating mystery and curiosity between them.

Tanya also realized that she needed time alone to do nothing. This made her more interested in contact with Gary when he was available. Their men and women friends encouraged them to talk about difficult but important subjects, like gender differences in their attitudes toward sex, money, and intimacy.

People like Tanya and Gary often crush the mystery out of friendship and sexual love because they cannot bear the inevitable uncertainty involved. We never know other people unless we honor their independence. Tanya and Gary had to learn that they needed to spend some time alone or with friends. As they did, they deepened respect and curiosity for each other, both essential to sustaining intimacy over a lifetime.

In our unwillingness to face our aloneness, we look to our lovers to make us feel okay and build up our self-esteem. We demand of our sexual partners that they be friend, mother, father, mentor, buddy, confessor, and spiritual advisor, which is too much for any relationship. Self-esteem—that solid inner sense of who we are—comes not just from successful encounters with and approval from persons we are attracted to, especially sexually, but much more profoundly from same-gender acknowledgment and support from persons who are like us, particularly those who are older and admired by us.

Ultimately, of course, we *are* alone. We all have our own unique characteristics, our own essence, our own spirituality. And while we can experience oneness with the universe and with others, ultimately we return to our self. Learning to contain our secrets and live with a feeling of delight and privacy is crucial for intimacy.

Intimate sharing grows out of

- A sense of who you are
- Who the other person is
- How receptive each of you is feeling toward the other

- An awareness of the appropriateness of time and place.

We have all met people who, within the first ten minutes, tell us about their dysfunctional family and abusive childhood. We immediately sense that they habitually repeat the same story. Their confession in no way enhances intimacy. In fact, we feel bombarded and repelled.

When intimate relationships function like therapeutic relationships, the sexual bond and sense of mystery diminish. We even go so far as to encourage individuals and couples to eliminate the word *need* from their vocabularies. "Needs" are for children; adults have "wants" and "desires." Adults can be refused and disappointed, but *the only thing they really need is food, water, and shelter.* Too much disappointment can, and probably should, lead to eventual rejection. But a "no" here and there is acceptable and necessary. By accusing a lover of not meeting your needs, you turn him into a "bad parent." There is then an inevitable argument about whether this accusation is fair, an argument during which both parties can be cruel to the other. This interaction is hardly sexually enlivening.

Most women, for example, are not turned on by what scared little boys their men feel like inside. They have a certain amount of time and compassion for this kind of sharing, but when repeated a number of times it decreases the sexual allure. Men, however, need to explore those vulnerable parts of themselves, as evidenced by the pioneering work of Robert Bly, Sam Keen, and others.

We taught Gary and Tanya that when you share a secret with someone you are close to and that person handles it like a precious jewel, this renews the intimacy of first love, generating eros and excitement. At that moment, you are someone who is evolving, becoming someone new, like a butterfly emerging from a chrysalis.

Most couples do not treat each other with this sense of wonder and interest. Instead, they are struck in repetitive patterns that breed boredom. We encourage couples to take on an attitude of discovery, so their time together can become an adventure again.

This sense of wonder is a critical distinguishing feature of healthy individuals, who have a reverence for the immensity of life's mysteries. They bring a sense of wonder into their daily lives. Their relationships are exciting and enriching. In this way, the secrets of life are opportunities, not things to be dreaded.

The Power of Holding and Managing Our Secrets

All of the above examples deal with individuals striving to grow in terms of self-esteem, self-responsibility, and giving and receiving love. But they each lacked the skills and information we make available in this book. They were also unsure of the meaning and importance of their secrets.

We provided them with our Western set of tools and concepts. Other cultures have formalized rituals for encouraging personal vision and purpose. Eastern mystical traditions keep secret wisdom from the students until it is believed that an individual is ready to handle it with maturity. Our friend, Gigi Coyle, who leads "vision fasts" through Ojai, a growth center in California, believes that there is spiritual power in being carefully discriminating about whom to tell your secrets to and when to tell them. In a recent conversation with us, she said:

"There is no right or wrong about how to do things, but when people go on a vision fast with us, we do help them to make new choices about how to share that experience. A vision fast starts out as a group experience in the wilderness, but then the participants each go off by themselves for three or four days, without food, asking for a vision or visions to guide them in their lives. When the group gets back together, there is always the tendency to want to immediately tell each other what happened, but we ask that they hold their stories until the next day. This allows a time of integration and deepening before the story spills out. We also ask that the story be limited to twenty minutes. Often people think that they cannot possibly condense the most powerful experience of their lives into twenty minutes, but in the distillation process, they discover what was most germane, most critical to their experience. It is an important sifting process."

During their vision fast, most people learn to be comfortable with silence. This enables them to distinguish what is important to tell and whom to tell it to. If you are in the habit of repeatedly telling the same story, it becomes programmed and you miss the learning in the telling. When you listen inside and truly hear the appropriateness of telling a particular person, then you often learn something new from the telling. You learn from that person's reactions, and also from hearing yourself as you enter the reality of your story. New things come out, and things are revealed that you did not understand until you told your story in an appropriate way to an appropriate person.

How do you know with whom or when telling your secrets is appropriate? We use the Life Enhancement Grid.

Gigi uses a process called council, a Native American practice which teaches people to be comfortable with silence and to listen inside for the story that needs to be told in the moment, the story that comes from the heart. When we learn to listen to the quiet in our own hearts, we can distinguish the story that serves the self, community, and God all at once. When someone speaks from that place, no matter how tired the listeners may be, all will wake up, riveted by the power of the sharing.

One of the intentions of a vision fast is to bring gifts back to "your people." Who your people are is one of the questions that you take with you into the wilderness. When you share with someone who is part of your people, then both of you should be served, as well as God. Clearly deciding *who* to tell is as important as deciding *what* to tell.

Not every environment needs to be sacred ground in the way it is in traditional cultures. Nevertheless, we each need to have some sacred space in our lives to develop a strong personal sense of meaning and purpose. This gives us the strength to function effectively in the voyeuristic society we describe in the next chapter.

Secrets

	EXPLORATION	CATHARSIS	INDIVIDUATION
1. In the Soup	Life is unmanageable. I want to believe it is not so bad.	I begin to take responsibility: "My life is unmanageable."	I believe there is hope for me. I am willing to reach out for help.
2. Shame Keeps You Silent	I am not like others. What am I doing here? This does not apply to me.	I realize I am suffering and I need help, but I'm too ashamed to reach out.	I am alone with this, but I don't want to be alone anymore.
3. Telling the Secret	I am listening to others, but I still minimize my own pain.	I am afraid and overwhelmed by my emotions.	I begin to enjoy telling my secrets to others. I learn to bear my feelings.
4. The Telling Works	I find pleasure in feeling and in exploring my secrets.	I immerse myself in intense emotional work and witnessing others' pain.	I develop increased tolerance for feeling. I discover that I enjoy discussing my own and others' pain.
5. Stuck in the Telling	I share my pain with everyone. Only those who listen are my friends. But I'm also still unhappy.	I continue intense emotional work. I become aware of a different life, one driven by pleasure, not therapy.	I am responsible for my own life. What risks must I take to ensure fulfillment?
6. Secrets to Tell, Secrets to Keep	I learn to make choices based on what gives me pleasure. But I will not harm others as I pursue my pleasure.	I take risks. I succeed and fail. I accept pain as a natural part of life.	Some people like me, some don't. I choose my friends and my way of life.
7. Freedom	I discover detachment from life's successes and failures.	I value my feelings equally.	I accept death as a natural part of life, painful only to those left behind.

2

The Voyeuristic Society

In the spring of 1990, while publicizing our first book, *Emotional Healing,* Karen appeared on the *Oprah Winfrey Show.* For Karen, it was an exciting but excruciating experience. As a therapist, Karen wanted to declare that the one-shot catharsis of a television confession does not substitute for the hard work of emotional healing. Yet, as an expert, she was called on by Oprah to assess each person's problem quickly and provide "solutions" for the audience about problems that never would have been discussed publicly ten years ago.

KAREN: "There were ten other people on the 'panel.' I was the only expert. Everyone else had either abandoned their children or been abandoned by their parents. Oprah moved quickly from guest to guest extracting deeply personal stories of childhood suffering. Amazingly, the guests complied with Oprah's psychological probing, willingly baring their souls.

"I found myself torn between my dual agenda: to promote my book and to serve as the healer in this sea of emotional pain. Some of the suffering was quite raw, and some of it was buried under an assortment of rationalizations.

"Afterwards, I realized that I had become so caught up in pain and drama that I forgot to plug the book. When the show was over, I spent an hour backstage talking with five brothers and sisters abandoned by their mother at a bus station eighteen years before. Being on the show had opened them up, but had done nothing to resolve their pain. They were in shock and needed help. I am so glad that I was there and aware of it."

Are Oprah's guests and viewers with similar childhood traumas being helped? Is the audience learning how to understand and aid those who have experienced such trauma? Of course not. Everyone—guest, expert, host, audience—is part of a spectacle. Unaware of appropriate psychological self-disclosure, guests discuss aspects of their private lives that should only be shared in a sacred space. What Karen and the millions of Oprah's viewers saw instead was pseudotherapy, with the guests driven by what we call an addiction to excitement. Ultimately, such inappropriate confessing not only makes a person feel worse but also misleads the public about the difficult nature of therapeutic work.

As an audience, are we inspired to tell our secrets? Or are we left thinking we don't have the serious problems of television guests? Is Oprah's show a voyeuristic culture's *Queen for a Day,* where others' misery frees us from carefully considering our own lives? As an article in the *New Yorker* (August 10, 1992) commented:

It's not that we were fascinated by any of the stories or psychodramas that the guests on these shows were relating; it's more that we couldn't quite believe that people would actually go on television to discuss the stuff. We said to ourselves over and over again "Who cares?" and yet we kept watching. We told ourselves that this allowed us a direct view into the American psyche—that by tuning in to "Sally Jesse Raphael" and "Donahue" and "Jane" and "Geraldo," we were able to learn certain basic truths about this nation we live in. But when we tried to decide exactly what those little pearls of insight were, we couldn't. Mostly, we just became more and more aware of our own voyeurism.

These shows have therapy "experts" who, along with the host, encourage this kind of soul-bearing. The expert's presence conveys that telling secrets is good, and that real change is possible for the participants and the audience. We don't buy it.

What happens to these guests after the show? We hope for the best, but the healing process requires a longer journey, more like two steps forward, one step back. And it involves getting things off one's chest, not only by telling the story but also by *experiencing* the related emotions. Aristotle called this catharsis.

A therapeutic environment enables a person to have this flooding of feelings about a past event. Eventually the person is released from trauma, but only after repeated cathartic experiences. Without a supportive therapeutic environment, the benefits of a catharsis are short-lived. A new beginning can mean quickly recycling old behavior. As we said in the last chapter, divesting ourselves of our solitary pain brings us closer to others and to a deeper acceptance of ourselves. But this rarely happens in the voyeuristic society.

History of the Voyeuristic Society

We think that the national spectacle of Jacqueline, John, and Caroline Kennedy's grief at President John F. Kennedy's funeral marked a turning point in legitimizing the media's right to invade the emotional lives of others. Before that time, usually emotions were depicted only on television in dramatic series or soap operas. News programs and the few talk shows on the air, like *Today,* concentrated on public events.

There were a few exceptions to this norm. In the 1950s, women competed for money and prizes by presenting stories of misery on *Queen for a Day.* Personal histories were told, but always in a favorable light, on *This Is Your Life.* Edward R. Murrow assailed Joseph McCarthy's character when he rebuked the senator's efforts to expose "communists" in all walks of life. But, in general, respect for privacy prevailed.

The Kennedy assassination altered this media orientation. We believe that the emotional catharsis that the nation underwent broke down the boundary between public and private. People's legitimate concern with the activities of the President's widow and her children degenerated over the years into what political scientist Larry Sabarto has called a feeding frenzy. The public seemed to have an unending desire to know *everything* about the Kennedys. This preoccupation soon spilled over to other celebrities and average citizens.

The Vietnam War expanded this national impulse. Television brought the horrors of war—which in the past had been only familiar to soldiers—into the living room. The personal stories of soldiers and protesters tore at the hearts of all Americans.

The assassinations of Malcolm X, Martin Luther King,

and Robert Kennedy added to the explosion of public grieving. Who could not be touched by the pictures of Malcolm's widow, the mournful march of blacks and whites to bury Dr. King, and the agonizing pictures of Robert Kennedy lying on the ground, his head cradled in a political supporter's lap, life ebbing from him moments after his greatest political victory?

Two other events fueled the voyeuristic society. The first was Watergate. The exposure of a vast conspiracy to obstruct justice that reached into the White House—resulting in jail sentences for cabinet members and presidential assistants, and the resignation of President Nixon—shook the nation's belief in its institutions and in the people sworn to protect and defend the Constitution. Cynicism spread. Now everyone could be suspected of a hidden agenda of self-promotion, private gain, or illicit activities.

The second event that pushed the voyeuristic society forward was the creation of *60 Minutes,* the elder statesman of reality-based television. *60 Minutes* developed investigative reporting into a dramatic form that pitted a star reporter against a wrongdoer who either refused to cooperate or confessed in front of the cameras. Over the years, this form of journalism spread, mixed with ever more sensationalized approaches. Now, on a daily basis, viewers can see scandal and sin exposed on such shows as *Hard Copy, A Current Affair, Unsolved Mysteries, 20/20,* and on and on.

By the 1980s the voyeuristic society had taken hold. Technological advances allowed instant transmission. Ted Turner's CNN was broadcasting news twenty-four hours a day. Talk shows, which had once centered on actors promoting upcoming movies, cooking demonstrations, and comedy and musical sketches, were focusing exclusively on the darkest secrets of humanity and the oddest kinds of human behavior. On any given day, viewers could see programs featuring child abuse, alcoholism, rape, and transvestism. In one typical week, topics included two women married to the same man without knowing it, a woman who had nineteen operations to look like a Barbie doll, a couple whose engagement was on hold because a psychic said the future husband was cheating, and a married couple in which the husband was sixty-two years older than his wife. As topics became more sensationalized, ratings soared. And with that, talk shows proliferated.

This successful format crossed over to other media. Voyeuristic magazines flourished, led by *People,* the *National Enquirer,* and the *Star.* Newspapers, traditionalists by nature, yielded to the movement by featuring celebrity news and gossip, and relentlessly pursuing the private lives of public officials. Movie and record stars, such as Madonna, willingly exposed their private lives, their bodies, and their innermost fantasies.

By the early 1990s there seemed to be no limits at all. In today's voyeuristic society, we live by the principle that inquiring minds have a *right to know.* If you do not tell all, the media assumes you are hiding something heinous. Nowhere was this new code more evident than in Gary Hart's failed presidential run in 1988. Hart challenged the media to find any evidence of personal wrongdoing. Within days, he was exposed as a philanderer and forced to drop out of the race. Only thirty years previously, Jack Kennedy had regular extramarital contacts that were well known to the press but were never discussed. Now, the press believes its duty is to hold our leaders to standards that few in our society can live up to.

Bill and Hillary Clinton felt the full fury of the voyeuristic society while campaigning in the New Hampshire primary. Their insistence on their right to marital privacy saved his presidential campaign from disaster. This was a rare occasion. Much more common was the media exposure of facts like Liberace's homosexuality and his death by AIDS, even though he did not wish this information known. Nor did Arthur Ashe want his life disrupted by the public display that he had become HIV-positive from a blood transfusion. But his privacy was not respected. Ashe, to keep a newspaper from breaking the story, called his own press conference to release the information. One of the most extreme examples of the voyeuristic impulse is the practice called outing, whereby gay-rights activists expose gays in prominent position in government or business.

We agree that the exposure of hypocrisy is justified on the grounds that our heroes and role models ought to tell the truth. Watergate taught us all that lesson. What we question is the relish with which we as a society savor these scandals. Do we enjoy that the mighty have fallen, or is it, in fact, a *pain-avoidant* pleasure that masks the misery of our own lives and the pain of our own secrets?

When we hold our heroes to such standards that they cannot be forgiven, we don't encourage openness, because we are not supporting a culture that believes a person can learn from mistakes. Rigid standards of decency offer the opportunity to be hateful or at least obnoxiously self-righteous: "We are better than you because we would never make that mistake."

In contrast to this voyeurism, consider the position of the president of a foundation that supports research on Huntington's disease, an as yet incurable illness, deadly to some and only carried in the genes of others. During a national public radio broadcast, she acknowledged that she had the disease in her family history but had decided to keep to herself the information about whether she was to have the disease later in life or was only a carrier. She believed her message would be diluted if the news story focused on her personal concerns. We think she is right.

The problem in the voyeuristic society is not only the demand that all must be told, but also the distorted way we have learned to hear things. Telling a secret requires a level of responsibility by the teller that is more profound than mere entertainment value. The president of the Huntington's Disease Society wants people to care about her cause, not herself, so she chooses to keep her situation private. Information is a commodity that citizens in a democratic society should have access to. But do we, as individuals, have the emotional maturity to handle it with respect and care?

The Voyeuristic Impulse

Given the national rush toward voyeurism, what is it psychologically that people get out of this kind of experience? For us, the voyeuristic impulse has two aspects: one good, the other bad. The good aspect is the excitement of sharing the drama of other people's lives. This draws us to books, the theater, and the movies. The second impulse is insidious: the desire to numb ourselves and feel better than others. Once you address your own inner life, fascination with others' stories diminishes dramatically. You don't care less about others, but the caring is no longer serving to distract you from your own pain.

Viewers need to realize that what they are watching is not "real life," but "images" manufactured by some people for "consumption" by others. Each show involves editing, camera work, scripting, and dramatic pace. We watch pictures of how others believe things are, not necessarily how they actually are.

Paralleling the media's manipulation of reality is the manipulation that occurs among the guests who create images so as to appear on television. A person's image rarely mirrors reality. When you portray yourself to others according to an image, you must carefully manage that image. As you do, you betray yourself and undermine your capacity to be intimate, which is the *ability to present one's true inner life and expression in the presence of another.*

Image management moves relentlessly from television into the inner life. Edward and Louise exemplify a couple whose relationship was destroyed by images. They had been dating for a few months when we met them. They thought they were emotionally close, but, in fact, they found little satisfaction in their relationship.

Edward and Louise were playing the image management game with each other. They wore Armani clothes, read *Vogue* and *GQ,* drove a Lexus and a BMW, and dined out at least three times a week at the trendiest restaurants. Both had good administrative jobs that allowed them financial freedom. They appeared cool, sophisticated, and independent.

Privately they acknowledged that they could see the other's secrets behind his or her mask, but neither realized that the other was aware of this. Edward had been diagnosed as a manic depressive in college. He had been off medication for several years but was finding it hard to maintain his equilibrium while in a troubled relationship. Ironically, Louise's father had numerous hospitalizations for mental illness. Louise had been embarrassed by this situation throughout her childhood.

Edward and Louise believed that to tell the truth would disappoint the other party and destroy their relationship. To us, however, their relationship disguised fear and was doomed to failure. The more Edward and Louise tried to manage their secrets, the more hurt they felt, imagining the other party did not care. They wanted the impossible—intimacy without vulnerability.

More and more, image making, not intimacy, is the central task of people in the voyeuristic society. This is as true for Madonna as for the guests on television talk shows. We believe that many guests create an image as "sufferer" or "victim" based on the images they have previously seen on television. What show is dramatically satisfying without tears? What a failure the guest would feel like if he or she didn't break down. In fact, while recently "channel surfing" we saw an amazing scene—on three different talk shows, on three different channels, all three guests were crying!

Voyeurism can become pathological when a person believes his or her image *is* reality. An example is Jennifer, twenty-five, who works as a personal trainer at a local health club that caters to powerful executives and their wives. As part of her job, Jennifer often hears "confessions" from the people she helps get into shape. Jennifer enjoys this aspect of her work, being a devoted fan of television soap operas and gossip magazines. Jennifer is so caught up with other people's lives that she ignores her own obvious problems.

JENNIFER: "Every time my boyfriend George told me he was tired or too busy to see me, I'd believe him. George had an important job and talked with such authority. I was so involved with George that I stopped seeing my friends even when I was free. I talked everything over with him. I would be hurt later when I found out that he had not been listening."

Jennifer was unable to engage in other relationships when her boyfriend was not around. Yet, she could have a relationship with George that was largely based on fantasy. Jennifer's way of living exemplifies one of the most shocking aspects of the voyeuristic society—that is, when we are "in on the secrets" of so many others, to have real contact with and accurate information about friends and lovers becomes more and more irrelevant.

Voyeurism is also harmful because it is a form of addiction. People addicted to voyeurism are driven by excitement. Living a life based on this kind of "excitement," in turn, is fueled by what we have called adrenaline rushes. In *Emotional Healing,* we observed that many adult children of alcoholics or of abusive homes are hooked on adrenaline to manage the stress they unconsciously but consistently created for themselves. The voyeuristic society supports this life-addicted lifestyle. When you have real problems, get interested in other people's lives. Turn on the TV. Read *People* magazine. All of this is better than dealing with your own pain and disappointment about real relationships.

Voyeurism can take on the three aspects of addiction:

- *Compulsion:* We do it out of habit, not even imagining a way of life where we are not immersed in someone else's story.
- *Tolerance:* We get "high" when we have a good

story to sink our teeth into. But if we've already heard it before, it doesn't have the same level of satisfaction.

- *Dependency:* If, for some reason, we are removed from our voyeurism, we then find it hard to feel normal and take satisfaction from what is actually going on around us.

The addiction to excitement becomes *compulsive* when we look forward to the latest revelation of public gossip, as if the content of *People* magazine or *Entertainment Tonight* actually enriches the quality of our lives. The addict then develops a tolerance to this outside stimuli so that the most recent, outrageous revelation becomes commonplace. *Dependency* develops when we find ourselves anxious and bored because we do not have this input.

Let's look at how this was played out in one woman's life. Andrea, forty-two, had struggled for years with an increasing coldness that she felt toward her husband, John. Her low sex drive was in sharp contrast to his. Female friends empathized with her situation, exchanging hostile humor about insensitive men obsessed with "the act." Even though the marriage was troubled, Andrea's two children—a son in high school and a daughter in college—were doing well. She had a busy, if not lucrative, career as a craftsperson making glass earrings.

Andrea's life felt precarious but manageable until John announced he wanted to separate. Upon hearing John's wishes, she went numb. The reality of this change did not set in for several months. Andrea coped by becoming more involved with her work. However, as the months passed, Andrea noticed that she had become the focus of her friends, a specimen to be dissected with care, not a person to be included in gatherings.

ANDREA: "I did not like feeling like an alien creature so I started to isolate myself. When my friends called me, they wanted to hear about *my* dates and what I was doing with *my* time. I believe they care about me and wish me well, but I got this creepy feeling that they were watching a movie. My friends sounded like they were readers of *People* magazine. When I asked about their lives they said they were routine. I knew I was living out their fantasies."

Andrea's experience was a nightmare. Not only did she suffer the pain of abandonment by her husband, but also she had become an object of voyeurism. And what did Andrea feel? Shame. She felt that her friends had turned on her and that she no longer belonged. Their voyeurism took its toll.

Voyeurism thus triggers a rush of adrenaline, a drug we cannot live without, but one that can make a sensible life seem mundane and irrelevant. Disregarding the adventure that exists in a life lived wholeheartedly can lead to the addictive process of voyeurism.

From a Voyeuristic Society to a Healing Society

In many urban and educated communities, if you haven't been in psychotherapy, you are suspected of being defensive and unwilling to be introspective. Our culture is not mature enough to handle the enormous change implicit in the new values of openness. We applaud the many ways people are coming together. Intentional communities are a wonderful replacement for the vacuum left by the breakdown of the closeness that was once fostered by neighborhoods, churches, and other local organizations. As our society becomes more mobile, we need to build affiliation quickly and effectively into our lives, but we also need to come to grips with the value of privacy in this environment of shared secrets. Voyeurism can be really harmful when a person is isolated by a secret or when people do not have the tools or time to help create healing around a revelation.

We met Betty, a thirty-year-old bookkeeper at a furniture sales company, after her supervisor, Tom, tried to intervene in an abusive relationship. Betty had shown up on four different occasions with bruises on her face. After the last time, Tom called Betty into his office. He told Betty that she had become the major source of conversation in the office and that he wanted to help her. He suggested that they see us.

Betty was dismayed by her boss's comments and by her fellow employees' awareness of her problems. Because she feared losing her job, she agreed, reluctantly, to visit us. While Tom waited outside, Betty admitted to abuse at the hands of her boyfriend. But she also expressed rage at her boss and coworkers. Although we tried to intervene quickly, Betty's feelings of being a voyeuristic object got in the way. She never came back to us and quit her job that week. Talking to therapists overwhelmed her with shame.

If Tom had talked with his employees about their feelings, Betty might have been able to handle getting help. Would a referral to resources that specialized in battered women have been better than referring her to health professionals? We think so, but this is an afterthought. Talking with someone with whom you can identify, who has been through the difficult transition of separating from an abuser, is different from talking to a curious party who you feel might be raising the question of your sanity.

Confronting the problem of the voyeuristic society is not unlike riding a razor's edge. On one side, it is enjoyable to be entertained by other people's melodramas, and it can provide a personal catharsis. The insidious other side is that watching shames the sharer and distances the viewer from the experience. Rarely then does it lead to healing.

For example, Karen experienced both sides of this issue with her stories about her cancer treatment. She used them as a teaching tool in a lecture, and then found herself deluged with anecdotes about cures brought about by different treatment methods than the ones she had chosen. Hearing Karen's self-disclosures made others think they were more intimate with her than they actually were. She did not ask for their ideas, which, in fact, rekindled concerns about choices she had already made. She recognized that people were only trying to be helpful, but they were not able to see that they were returning her secrets to her in a form that caused her more distress: they planted "shoulds" and "could haves" in her mind simply because they could not sit quietly with the enormity of her secret without trying to help.

Doing Your Own Emotional Healing First

The response to Karen illustrates why people must do their own emotional work before they can be present to hear another person's secrets. Without such work, usually a person cannot avoid feeling and acting voyeuristically.

Inhibitions and social sanctions that formerly kept people from speaking up about themselves are breaking down. We are thrilled that victims of abuse—mothers against drunk drivers, beating victims, and children who are hurt and neglected—are finding ways to open up the truth of their suffering. In the past, such people feared retaliation for telling their secrets, or feared they wouldn't be believed.

Telling secrets makes us vulnerable and can alienate us from those who listen if we tell too much or if listeners don't respond the way we wish. We must be clear about our personal boundaries: what feels all right to tell, when and to whom, and what we hope to gain by the telling. But this, unfortunately, has become far more difficult as the therapeutic community has joined hands with our society's voyeuristic impulses.

3

The Failure of
the Therapeutic Movement

When Andy first came to see us, he had been sober for one year and was ending a destructive three-year relationship. Thirty years old, a substitute teacher, Andy was active in Alcoholics Anonymous (AA) and worked out daily. As a result, he was developing a modest faith in the future and an athletic body. Yet, he spoke negatively about himself and was unsure if he could live without his girlfriend. They had "gotten sober together," but had recently split up. Each had felt exhausted trying to work things out, and they had mutually decided to separate. Being alone, however, made Andy very anxious.

Another fact also stood out at our initial interview: Andy could not stop talking about his childhood and his relationships with women. He seemed desperate to get involved again. As his therapy progressed, Andy developed some self-confidence, and began to date. As he did, Andy realized he had no idea how to be with people outside a therapeutic environment.

Andy's feelings that he was worthless and uninteresting increased proportionally to how attracted he was to a woman. To cope, he talked to women about his childhood and past problems, or he praised therapy and AA. Initially, Andy's self-revelations intrigued women. Boredom, however, soon replaced fascination. In turn, Andy would jettison women if they matched him problem for problem. Andy didn't really want a relationship with someone who was equally needy. He found himself spending more and more time at AA, using it as a social club rather than a way to continue his healing.

Andy, like many of our clients, could be called a therapy junkie, stuck in the self-disclosing phase of emotional healing. For him, opening up in a therapeutic environment was such a breakthrough that he thought intimate self-disclosure was a way of life. Divesting ourselves of our solitary pain *does* bring us closer to others and to a deeper acceptance of ourselves. What it doesn't do, though, is encourage a person to separate out the work of healing from the task of living a fulfilling life.

For example, when Andy faced presenting himself in everyday situations, he imagined things about others that made him anxious—for example, that people thought he was "stuck-up" because he was tall and well built. Eventually, Andy realized that his immaturity did not disappear as he became more comfortable with his secrets. He needed to learn how to live a life focused on fulfillment and pleasure.

But this was not easy given his background. Andy had a childhood filled with physical abuse and parental lying and criticism. Andy coped by using drugs and alcohol to obliterate the past. When Lady Macbeth dealt with the secret of Banquo's murder, she wandered the halls of her castle trying to wash the unseen blood from her hands. Similarly, even after Andy became sober, he could not get his father's harping, negative messages out of his mind. Acknowledging and talking about his humiliation and shame was critical to Andy's sense of well-being, but this kind of discussion had to be done in a sacred space, not over a romantic dinner or on a television talk show.

In this chapter we distinguish what a therapeutic environment is and what it is not, exploring its benefits and drawbacks, and the danger that now exists because too many people expect that the *special friendship* and *controlled intimacy* provided by a therapist or a self-help organization can also be found in life.

The Power of the Unconscious

Sigmund Freud made the momentous discovery that the unconscious directs our thoughts and our actions. Moreover, he said the more traumatic the memories and experiences repressed in the unconscious are, the more likely the unconscious directs us in self-destructive ways. Freud's therapeutic approach suggests that by exploring the unconscious, irrational impulses can be replaced by conscious choices.

Carl Jung added the idea that the unconscious takes on shapes called archetypes that must be integrated into the conscious for one to become fulfilled as a person, or "individuated." Jung also talked of the "shadow"—all the aspects of our personality that we reject as unacceptable. Without such acceptance, we see our faults in others.

Wilheim Reich contributed the physiological perspective to the study of the unconscious. He suggested that a person's ability to function in a healthy fashion was limited by the level of vitality of the body and its capacity for feeling. He argued that a person could not change until the body was more alive with feeling, despite efforts to make the unconscious available through insight.

The fourth major therapeutic breakthrough was comprised of the behavioral and cognitive approaches pioneered by J.B. Watson, B.F. Skinner, and Arnold Lazarus. They viewed the unconscious as an artificial contruct that should be ignored, favoring the study of specific thoughts and actions that could be modified by careful intervention.

In all four therapeutic approaches, the mandate is to "tell all" so therapy can be appropriate and effective. Telling secrets enables a person to make changes in his or her life. In the therapeutic relationship, the "healer" has enormous power. Improved mental health involves a change in mood—for example, the lifting of a depression—and an alteration in how one thinks about problems or reacts to stressful situations. Let's see how the traditional approach can be used.

Adelle had a secret that she had repressed for many years without having to face any consequences. At forty years old, she was a successful computer technician, married, and had a twelve-year-old daughter, Mallory. Adelle became curious about the Adult Children of Alcoholics (ACOA) movement because her own family history had been grim. Adelle's father had died from chemical poisoning when she was eight. Her mother was alcoholic, but no one outside the family ever knew. Adelle had become very good at keeping secrets and "making nice" as she put it. When Adelle was eighteen, she escaped to college on a scholarship. Pretty and charming, Adelle became "the girl men wanted to marry," receiving three marriage proposals by the age of twenty-three, when she finally accepted a proposal from George. Although she was unaware of it, she had secrets that even she did not know.

After attending several of our workshops and entering individual psychotherapy, Adelle sorted through the facts of her life. As she put them together, Adelle realized that her father must have killed himself. His colleagues covered up this tragedy so that she and her mother would receive the death benefits from an "industrial accident."

She shared her discovery with us, but decided to not raise it with her mother. That relationship already had enough pain, Adelle concluded. However, the catharsis that resulted from Adelle's discovery led to a sense of peacefulness, of letting go of the desire to be perfect.

Adelle used the therapeutic environment for the right purpose: to heal. Discovering the secret of her father's suicide was critical to her, but she did not let the healing of old wounds get in the way of enjoying the life she had built over the years. The ability to repress became transformed into an ability to set her memories aside and get on with her life in a more healthy way.

The therapeutic mandate to tell all to those you are entrusting with your healing is not transferable to other relationships. However, over the past twenty-five years this is precisely what has happened in our society.

The Roots of Confusing the Therapeutic Boundary

We trace the idealization of the therapeutic relationship back to the late 1960s, a time of exploration, experimentation, and rebellion. Rebellion toward authorities took place in mental health as well. At that time, the idea that the therapist had some special charisma or knowledge became highly suspect.

This suspicion powered three important *self-help* movements: (1) AA and other twelve-step groups; (2) workshop "technologists," the most famous being Dale Carnegie, who figured out ways to package social skills, self-esteem, and other enriching adult education topics; and (3) humanistic psychology pioneered by Carl Rogers, Abraham Maslow, and many others.

The proliferation since the 1960s of AA and related groups throughout the world occurred because their techniques work. Their motto is: "You keep your sobriety by giving it away to others." Perhaps the best word for this form of self-help is *mentoring*. Individuals help others by being available directly (through sponsorship), by sharing their own recovery stories, and by reinforcing the norms of the group as a whole—sometimes called the fellowship. The benefits of belonging to a healthy community are accelerated by the encouragement of and example set by other members of the group.

Workshop technologists, like Dale Carnegie, and more recently people like Werner Erhard and Anthony Robbins provide the context and the information necessary for individuals to help themselves and become more effective in their lives. More importantly, these trainers have developed techniques to provide this information experientially rather than simply through lectures. Dale Carnegie, for example, is best remembered for helping people learn public speaking. But his more profound lesson was building the self-esteem of his course participants by giving them positive experiences of themselves in front of highly supportive coparticipants.

Humanistic psychology grew out of the mental health system itself. In the 1950s and 1960s treatment began to include prescribing antidepressant, antianxiety, and antipsychotic medications. In academia, psychology had shifted away from psychoanalysis to the study of what was statistically measurable in behaviors, attitudes, and cognitive processes. Humanistic psychology, based on the belief that people had the potential for growth and transcendental experiences, had begun at about the same time but had little academic support. Proponents of this form of psychotherapy believed help did not require extraordinary expertise and professional distance but rather social skills and an open heart.

Carl Rogers, a pioneer of the movement, presented a new model for the therapeutic relationship which had three major components. First, he argued for a sense of simple goodwill from the therapist to the client, what he called *unconditional positive regard*. This notion diverged from the objective and distant analyst who never chatted with a patient. The value of a therapist demonstrating that he or she likes and cares for a patient may be obvious today, but it was quite unusual when originally proposed. It was considered unscientific and thought of as sexually seductive.

Second, Rogers thought the therapeutic relationship should be cooperative. Together, the therapist and client explored resistance to the client's unconscious secrets. The therapist was instructed not to do anything other than to hear exactly what the client said and feed that information back, often verbatim. Healing occurs when the client has shared a secret and has been heard. This creates cathartic relief and a sense of having done something important.

The third component of this client-centered therapy was *how* the therapist listened to the client. Rogers recommended that the therapist *empathize* with the client, and express that empathy in words and tone. Specifically, Rogers asked therapists to discover themselves in the other person and to express that they understand what the client is going through because they are like the client. This is a gift to the client because it relieves him or her of a sense of isolation. Rogers believed this approach deepened feelings because two people are mutually empathizing with the pain that was originally the client's alone. Catharsis is thus more profound.

Once a person has worked with an empathetic listener, the distant, objective witness seems harsh and uninterested. Little wonder that this therapeutic movement took off. It's similar to having had the taste of fresh brewed coffee and then being forced to go back to instant—you would only do it if you were convinced that it would be "better" for you in the long run. In our experience, few people do.

The humanistic revolution brought a big change to the practice of psychotherapy because Rogers's approach demystified the relationship between healer and client. This set the stage for the explosion of self-help movements that then occurred. Who needs someone with a Ph.D. to listen carefully when a friend or acquaintance is available who has a similar traumatic past and for whom you feel warmth?

Personally, we applaud the virtues of Rogers's approach and believe his three principles are essential to creating sacred space for our clients. Nevertheless, we contend that the healing process needs to be supplemented by tools from other psychotherapeutic movements and from Eastern and indigenous spiritual traditions. Without these tools, Rogers's deprofessional approach can degenerate into a confessional relationship.

Let's look at an example of a proper therapeutic approach. Candace was twenty-two when she went for therapy. She knew what she had to talk about, but was too scared for several weekly sessions to share her secret, which was that Candace's father had sexually abused her from the age of six to age thirteen. She had never told anyone. But as she experienced therapeutic empathy, in this case with a male therapist, Candace ventured into the abyss of self-disclosure, slowly sharing the specifics of what had happened to her. While her relief was profound, Candace needed to focus on these events, repeatedly and painstakingly for the next three years. At that point, she felt confident enough to join a support group of other women who had been similarly abused. If Candace had shared the knowledge of her incest with friends before this point, they may have taken her side unconditionally, which would have been all to the good. But the task of healing her relationships with her father and with men in general would have been a much harder and longer ordeal because the feelings she had were far more complex than simple rage.

What was hard for Candace was that she continued to love and be grateful toward her father, who had been warm and caring to her throughout this period of therapy. By exploring her secrets, Candace brought the hidden facts to the surface and freed herself of childlike distancing behaviors that appeared irrational in her current adult life. Candace had buried her rage to protect the bond she had with her father. Unfortunately, this rage would surface and be directed at anyone else who came close.

Therapeutic empathy required accepting Candace's ambivalence, knowing that slowly her rage would emerge, and providing her with the sense of personal power and autonomy that her father's abuse had denied her. She built the psychological strength to confront her father and to eventually create an intimate relationship with a caring man.

Other Important Features of Sacred-Space Therapeutic Environments

Therapeutic environments offer other important features that help in healing. They

• Enable people to have a temper tantrum, express a murderous rage, and sob convulsively. These are all part of the expressive repertoire of emotionally healthy individuals, but they are rarely feelings for public exposure. A therapeutic environment is a safe place to increase your "emotional aliveness" by feeling these deep emotions. They may be childlike feelings, but it is not childish to feel them.

• Increase self-awareness, giving individuals more freedom to make choices, while diminishing fear of the unconscious. Having insight into your own and others' behavior gives you confidence.

• Help people learn how to give and receive feedback, essential for enhancing self-awareness. When you talk about feelings, healthy choices can be made. With practice, your ability increases dramatically.

• Support the discovery of personal boundaries and ways of healing. Clarity about what is and is not your responsibility gives you greater ability to not become a victim of others.

• Promote hearing and having faith in a person's "inner voice." The inner voice knows what is right for you. Following it leaves no regrets, even if it leads to calamity on occasion. A life of integrity is now possible.

• Encourage risk taking. With encouragement and support, you develop your abilities to make choices and take chances.

In turn, clients expect therapists and twelve-step groups to

• Be dedicated to seeing the best in the clients
• Confront clients when their behavior is self-defeating
• Have the clients' best interests at heart, rather than the therapists'
• Listen to clients in a nonjudgmental way
• Have no particular stake in what clients do or don't do

When secrets are shared in this environment, they have enormous emotional power. This allows a flooding of feeling, a relief to the heart, and a sense of having done something important and of spiritual significance.

The Danger of Therapeutic Relationships

In therapeutic situations, people express loyalty and grati-tude to therapists and group members. To have your se-crets known is a gesture of great trust, but it also leads to a dependence on others. When people entrust their se-crets to others and ask for help, they rely on an authority. This invokes dependence but also reenacts the primary dependence on parents and caretakers. In our experi-ence, initially this dependence is often constructive. When you have been traumatized, emotional healing requires facing and reexperiencing the pain that you couldn't bear as a child.

Zanda's therapeutic experience, for example, was a very positive one. Twenty-eight years old, bright, multi-lingual and attractive, Zanda seemed to have everything going for her, but she lived in fear and anxiety whenever a man came into her life.

ZANDA: "If I were a teenager, you would call me boy crazy, but I'm twenty-eight. I can't decide what clothes to wear, what present to buy, or even enjoy being out with my female friends. I can't stop thinking about whatever man I'm going out with. I worry about where he is and whom he's with. Men quickly decide that I *am* crazy, particularly after I rage at them over some little thing. Then they're gone."

Entering psychotherapy was a courageous choice for Zanda. She didn't know what she was afraid of until, after several sessions, she found herself "melting" right in the office. Her excitement and fear were paralyzing. She realized that if Terry approached her sexually, she would not be able to say no.

Zanda shared her feelings with Terry. He told Zanda to relax, breathe, and allow the feelings to flow through. Quickly she understood that her longing was not sexual at all, but that of a little girl who was overwhelmed with grief. She cried during session after session.

Abandoned emotionally by her mother and physi-cally by her father, Zanda had only known how to be close through eroticism, either by talking about "boys and sex" with her girlfriends or by playing out her sen-sual dreams with boys and men. Now, with Terry, she expressed her anger and sadness about her life.

After a number of therapy sessions, Zanda began to make many more healthy choices. Yet she still wondered if she could make it alone. She occasionally felt angry at how dependent she had become, but she was also grateful that she was successfully functioning in a new relationship and job.

Unlike the way Terry handled Zanda, many therapists believe they must reparent the wounded child inside their patient. This involves attempting to provide the unconditional love not given long ago. Not only is this impossible, but also it makes the client too dependent on the therapist, greatly increasing the danger of an abuse of power by the therapist, which we discuss below.

An effective healing process supports a client to acknowledge and express hidden pain and grieve deeply for the childhood that could have been. Zanda could not live her childhood over again, and the demands of the abandoned little girl were not doing her any good in the present.

The Power of the Healer

When there is little or no reciprocity in the self-disclosure of secrets, power inevitably flows to the one who listens. Whether a psychotherapist, a priest, a sponsor, or a friend, the helper can easily and even unconsciously take advantage of this power. The helper feels special in some way. Danger occurs when the helper and the helped believe that "specialness" is real rather than created by the person's dependence on the helper.

This is precisely what is happening in the voyeuristic society. Guests on talk shows believe that there is something special, not only in the circumstances, but also in the host. Oprah, Phil, Sally, and the other "gods" of television are seen as having a special power to examine explosive topics. Guests then allow themselves to be exploited just to have Phil or Oprah come over and hug or touch them.

In psychotherapy, this shift in power is reflected in feelings toward the therapist that mirror emotions, often buried in the unconscious, felt toward a person's parents. This is called transference. These feelings can be intensely positive, negative, and are usually both. They must be artfully explored so that secrets are revealed to the sharer as well as the listener.

As we saw in Zanda's story, the revelation of her inner chaos led to an intense dependence as she learned to sort out what her own personal choices were. If Terry had taken on the task of deciding what was right for her, the way a parent would, Zanda would not have had to learn to bear the pain when her own choices did not lead to success. Dysfunctional groups and healers do not want people to leave. Their role offers permanence to relationships between unequals, giving the "healer" a special role—a fantasy special friend on whom one can count, no matter what occurs. This dear friend is never judgmental and always takes your side. This is a highly unrealistic expectation and contrary to healthy adult functioning. Healthy people back away from situations that are injurious, seductive, or even simply not to their taste, whereas the desperate and hurt inner child, who could not leave an abusive situation in childhood, insists on making a destructive or impossible situation work.

The therapeutic injunction to do your best to see your client through to healing is a good one. Healers, however, become sick or die, relocate, or reach the limits of their ability to manage a relationship constructively. Healing is better served when clients leave on their own.

John Bradshaw offered a similar model for the family when he wrote in his book *On the Family* that "healthy families disintegrate in an orderly fashion." When one party is "special," he or she has trouble letting the other move away.

The dangers of specialness that exist within mental health professions also occur within religious groups and twelve-step fellowships, as well as in self-help courses like Weight Watchers and est. Anyone who leaves is a threat to the viability of the organization. Instead of dealing with that fear, the leaving individual is seen as "slipping" or not mature enough to take advantage of the value in the group.

Sometimes sexual relationships begin and grow within these communities. Some may turn out to be fulfilling and successful, but these relationships are all formed on the shaky foundation of a person's need for help. The current therapeutic mandate that "I'll be there for your problems and you be there for mine" inevitably devolves into taking turns being the demanding and dependent child. Extreme caution should be taken when forming sexual relationships within twelve-step fellowships. Healthy friendships and intimate relationships between adults exist for the pleasure of each other's company. They are between equals who are not looking for help from each other. Other reasons for closeness—such as security, habit, or economic interest—inevitably create problems down the road.

The Therapeutic Relationship in the Voyeuristic Society

Idealizing the therapeutic relationship is not surprising in the context of the voyeuristic culture. When the basis for friendships is the voyeuristic entitlement to know another's private thoughts and feelings rather than enjoying another's company, then it is natural to make the modus operandi of the relationship be self-disclosure.

Tragedy occurs, however, when the healing person turns on loved ones, complaining that these relationships are not as open and caring as the therapeutic ones. For example, a woman who falls in love with a male psychotherapist compares his sensitivity to that of her husband or lover. We witnessed the demise of a fifteen-year marriage of two friends of ours—Bob, a kind but quiet businessman, and Sylvia, an outgoing artist. Sylvia "outgrew" her husband while in therapy. She demanded that Bob become more "sensitive and artistic." Bob would not change. He liked himself and his life the way it had been. They soon parted.

The Paradigm of Self-Disclosure

Intimacy in a therapeutic environment is found in the feelings and thoughts that lie in a person's inner world. Intimacy rests on the ability to display one's inner life in ways that another person can understand. With time and experience, a healthy relationship encompasses closeness and separateness, and, above all, a deep and abiding respect for each other.

Our friends and loved ones should be open and trusting, but they are not our therapists, interested in hearing all our thoughts and feelings. We should not be allowed completely into each other's innermost experience, no matter how close we are to them. We must face our essential aloneness in the world, assuming personal responsibility for successes and failures, as well as having the courage to take unpopular actions because they are right.

When we accept our essential separateness, we meet others as unique people. Even if we have been married for years, or are parents of a twenty-five-year-old, the same sense of discovery applies. The mystery of life comes alive in this separateness and acceptance. When I tell you about my inner life, I am giving a gift that should be cherished by me and you.

We suggest that there is a need for a new paradigm of self-disclosure. This requires a level of self-esteem that develops naturally in a healthy home. Such a home has three primary characteristics:

• Parents are warm, loving, and accepting of the children
• The family expects the child ought to and can achieve realistic goals
• The family sees each individual as autonomous and distinct, so that parent-centered demands are not made on the children

In this new paradigm, emotional closeness pulsates like the heart and the breath, expanding and contracting. It has what biologists call "the involuntary" to it, because generally it cannot be controlled consciously. Rather, we let the closeness build, ebb and flow with interest and wonder. When we accept that there are natural shifts to relationships, we can calmly accept both deepening closeness and the natural process of distancing.

Closeness in this new paradigm can be seen in the sexual encounter. Some people want to be close all the time, to have no secrets, and to be in on the entire inner life of their loved ones. This is equivalent to overvaluing the moment of orgasm, where you are experiencing unity with your beloved, and potentially with the universe as a whole. You are forgetting all the time you have spent creating this moment and being fundamentally separate. In romantic notions of this idea, people want to die together like Romeo and Juliet. But these experiences are really small moments in a relationship. Huge blocks of time are spent being out in the world, which deepens interest and excitement.

In the healthy relationship, sexual and otherwise, you are respected, you accept your essential separateness and differences, and you are even appreciative of them. You take responsibility for expressing your own preferences. You also discover, with a sense of wonder, that your friend or lover does her or his best to accomodate you, within the limits of personal preferences.

Making the Shift

The therapeutic movement has empowered individuals who have felt powerless over their own actions and have been unable to express their preferences to their loved ones. As we shall see in the next chapter, there are incredibly valuable outside resources.

The therapeutic movement, by and large, however, has failed to move people out of the self-disclosure trap because it has allied itself with the media and the voyeuristic society in relentless pursuit of personal pain. A person's friends, sponsors, and therapists need to know when to get out of the way of the thriving, independent individual. What blocks this from happening is the fear that when people lose contact with their support system, they revert to their old behaviors, such as alcoholism, overeating, or robbing banks.

Underlying this fear are two extreme positions. One is that there is little possibility of change, so one must always be dependent on the therapeutic agent. The other is that once a person has told secrets in sacred space, he or she can live happily ever after. Instead, we believe there is a middle ground involving stages in the healing process that we discuss in chapter 4. This examination of the stages of healing needs to take place on a regular basis, as was the case with Wendy.

Wendy was forty-five, a mother of three grown children, and had successfully reentered the workforce as a marketing analyst after "the mommy-track years" during which her husband's salary supported the family. By most measures she was thriving, but she attributed this to having gone on retreats to "open the heart" to recharge, to reconnect with the sacred, and to exercise her emotional systems. She rarely in her daily life revisited memories of the beatings in her childhood by her older sister and the parental neglect that permitted this abuse of power. Still, the memories were important to her: these were the only parents and only childhood Wendy was ever going to have.

We often remember Wendy when we think about our work at Springhill, a spiritual retreat we founded with others, where we colead workshops entitled "Opening the Heart" with our friends Robert and Judith Gass. Wendy told us that once a year, she returned for a "spring housecleaning." All our workshops allow people to safely and expressively open up their full range of feelings in a sacred space. The premise of a Springhill workshop is simple: when you empty your heart of all the hurt, anger, and fear within a loving and supportive

community, you glimpse the possibility of turning negativity (e.g., anger, cynicism, judgmentalism) in your emotional life into a catharsis where old feelings are given
full expression and released from your heart.

Wendy's body remembered these opportunities for a
full expression and openness as if she were slowly carv-
ing a path through a dense forest by repeatedly walking
it. Retreats from the world, such as Springhill and our
workshops, give people like Wendy the opportunity, the
nurturing, and the support to unclog their emotional system. They also enable people to connect to the divine,
or, at least, the sublime. Delving into childhood secrets
with intense emotional expression keeps childhood bag-
gage out of current relationships. In addition, there are
often moments after an intense emotional release when
life tragedies take on spiritual meaning for the individual.
Wendy reported feeling grateful for her childhood because now she saw how her sense of independence and
capacity for perseverance were rooted in an upbringing
in which her own powerful resources had to be developed to get along.

One of the most important exercises we use in our
workshops is to invite our participants to respond to a
simple request made by an attentive witness over and
over again: "Tell me how you feel inside." A person's
responses may range from current concerns to early
childhood memories. The intensity and safety of the
workshop's environment invites and elicits emotional expression. When someone is sobbing deeply or raging,
your own feelings flow, though sometimes it's the desire
to tell another to shut up so you can think. This simple
act may sound silly, but it is a powerful assertion of self-
worth that one rarely expresses in nontherapeutic settings, where being polite is the priority.

Eventually, after taking several turns at being both witness and respondent, the workshop environment becomes a cauldron of feeling with no judgment attached—that is, murderous rage is not bad, sadness is not wrong, loving attachment is not good either. Healing begins in the discovery that the full spectrum of feeling is one's birthright. People can attain the capacity to love and to forgive those who have hurt them simply because those individuals and those experiences are an integral part of each person's unique life.

This experience of having one's heart open to the full range of human emotional experience, if only for a few moments on an occasional weekend, can inspire a person in the same way as witnessing a miracle. But a person must eventually come down from the mountain and go into the real world, where it is far more difficult to remain "enlightened." This part of the healing requires different, and far more practical tools. We introduce these tools in the next two chapters.

4

In and Out of the Soup

As we outlined in chapter 1, people pass through what we call the seven stages of emotional healing in their relationships to their secrets. By understanding these stages, you take a critical step toward healing the wounds caused by secrets. As part of this discussion we identify the intentions that fuel the behavior. Intention is crucial because the task of emotional healing is very hard. Without the strong intention to heal, the solution of simply burying one's secrets looks attractive during the early stages. At each stage, a three-phase process operates:

- *The Exploration:* This first phase involves examining family history and the unconscious motives for actions.
- *The Catharsis:* This phase shifts from awareness and memory to experiencing feelings of fear, hurt, rage, grief, and whatever other emotions surface. Many conflicting feelings emerge during this phase.
- *Individuation:* Individuation has been used in tra-

ditional psychological theory to refer to a time when one is fully healthy and separated from the familial ties that bind. We use the term to indicate that there are levels of individuation, expressed by increasing personal independence.

Before we take a closer look at these phases, let's discuss the seven stages. A summary of the stages and phases involved with secrets can be found at the end of chapter 1.

STAGE 1

In the Soup

In this stage, denial predominates. You live in the "it wasn't so bad" fantasy of life. You have forgotten much of the abuse that happened and do your best to escape from unpleasantness in the present. Family members don't talk to one another, sexual abuse remains a secret, birth secrets are not told, and you have little awareness of what you really feel about anything. Often, you still idealize your parents, rationalizing their problematic behavior as "It was just the way we did things." Even if you admit family life was hell, you don't know why and emphatically state, "It didn't affect me."

Your deepest feelings are masked by other feelings, so that grief is expressed through rage, hopelessness through bossiness, sadness through anger, guilt through blame, and low self-esteem through criticism. This masking distances you from painful emotions, enabling you to make sense out of senseless and crazy actions. In this way, you protect those responsible for having caused the problems.

In this stage, you have not begun the journey of emotional healing. In fact, you have no awareness that it is possible or even necessary. You tell yourself to forget the past and get on with your life. Although your life may be a mess, you don't understand that your problems could be of a psychological and emotional nature. Instead, you see self-defeating behaviors as a lack of discipline. If you recognize that you are repeating dysfunctional parental behavior, you assume that you are acting stupidly or irresponsibly, rather than accepting the inevitability of acting out unresolved family patterns.

The Intention: When people go into therapy while they are in this stage, their usual goals are simply to make their pain go away and to feel "happier." But their desire to change varies widely. They may show up for therapy and work hard at it. Then they may cancel their next three appointments. Sometimes feeling happy turns into self-punishment, because they fail to progress and return to being unhappy. The intention in this stage is inconsistent, unpredictable, and disorganized because it is painful to have to make the initial explorations of personal history with little sense of the rewards in the healing process that has been initiated.

STAGE 2

Shame Keeps You Silent

In this stage, you are aware of your secrets but feel so much shame about them that you can't tell anyone. Even in therapy your need to protect your positive childhood memories inhibits you from talking. Shame is the sense that you have no right to exist. It is not directly tied to a specific memory you feel bad about, which is guilt; rather shame is a way of life. Withheld opinions and emotions reflect shame when there is a sense of futility. For example, to believe that "self-expression makes no difference" reflects shame about what a person has to express. Shame differs from guilt because guilt presumes a sense of transgression for actions ("I am bad if I tell the secret"). The shame-filled individual is even prohibited from having a point of view ("The way I see things is bad because I am bad").

Shame develops naturally in a child when expressions and feelings are not encouraged, or, if they are, they are given little attention. It is attention to the inner life of a child that nurtures the development of a healthy self. The lack of it leads to shame. Violence and other boundary violations also inevitably cause shame. The victim believes he or she deserved such treatment. A shamed child, in turn, is further inhibited from developing a self because of the fear of further humiliation.

We saw this shame-based behavior at a recent workshop. Lilly, thirty-two, was very silent, almost invisible. She didn't have a partner for one of our exercises, so Karen paired with her. Lilly confessed to Karen that she felt alone and afraid. She told Karen, "I am still afraid of my mother and of my father, too. They always hurt me and my brothers, hitting us and shutting us outside in the shed sometimes for days at a time. Once my father broke my arm. I am ashamed of having parents like this. I don't want anyone to know. Before this workshop I always imagined that we were the only family like this. I believed everyone else had perfect parents. I don't know how to share my feelings. I don't think that I know what they are."

Lilly was just coming out of the "In the Soup" stage.

At our workshop she heard other people talk about their childhood. Although she didn't believe her parents' behavior was normal, she couldn't put it into perspective until she heard about other people's childhood. She dealt with her feelings by being strong and keeping her pain to herself. Lilly needed desperately to tell her secrets, and to have other people listen, care, and corroborate that she went through hell. But she struggled with her shame and her belief that it was wrong to reveal her secrets. Lilly was terrified that people would judge her harshly if they knew about her life.

For Angie the struggle was different. She knew her father's drunken beatings of her and her sisters were wrong, and she talked about it. Angie had trouble admitting, however, that her mother had repeatedly abandoned her and her sisters to her father's abuse. Angie needed to believe that she had one good parent. She idealized her mother, refusing to admit how neglected she was by her mother.

Both Angie and Lilly needed to discover the power of the healing process and to realize help did not carry the stigma of mental illness. Simply by being in the workshop, their healing process began as they listened to others and realized they were not alone. It was a big shift for them to even question their silence about their own families.

The Intention: Revealing the truth about your childhood within the confines of confidentiality is not about blaming. We don't want our clients to spend their lives punishing the perpetrators of childhood crimes. This is why intention is so importnant. Vengeance is a powerful motivation, but it must be examined in a therapeutic environment. Vengeance masks a deeper pain. The parents' hurt is passed on to the child, who later wants to give it back. When you're "In the Soup," that is all you can handle.

The intention in stage 2 is to stay in control as you explore your resistance to facing pain. In stage 2, your shame and your reactions to it must be exposed. Shame is slowly worked through by expressing rage at the people who shamed you in the safety of a confidential environment—for example, by pounding pillows, which allows people to express their rage at their parents.

Rage is a deeply personal statement that you have a right to an independent existence. This is not an intellectual discovery. Your body *rediscovers* it by psychodramatically pushing aggression to its natural limits. When you deny yourself a temper tantrum because you are inhibited or "don't feel it," you are expressing the same resistance to emotional health that a lethargic individual expresses toward exercise. Changing your physiological well-being requires repeated expression of feelings before rage flows authentically and unself-consciously.

STAGE 3

Telling the Secrets—Recovery Begins

In stage 3, sharing secrets begins to work. Deep grief and anger are expressed at parents, siblings, and caretakers who failed to nurture and care for you. For the first time, your feelings are accessible. As you recover, you overflow with emotion. At this point, you must share your feelings with appropriate people so as not to be isolated and alone. You begin to believe sharing is safe, and that caring and love exist for you. You begin to heal. It is a very exciting time.

Years ago at Springhill, a young woman named Nini came to our Opening the Heart workshop. She never left. For the next year, as she worked in the office and had private therapy sessions with another staff member, Nini cried and cried and cried. Whether we were planting the garden, bringing in firewood, celebrating someone's marriage, or taking out the mail, Nini would cry. She never cried alone, however. People put their arms around her and held her. Little groups would form, singing to her, rocking her gently, witnessing her pain and celebrating her healing. Eventually, when memories of the pain emerged less frequently, Nini stopped crying and started laughing. We still remember her melodious laugh. She was a woman of great courage who decided not to hide what she felt. All she needed was the time and permission to feel what she was feeling, and to be loved while she did it.

The Intention: Stage 3 is when the intention to heal involves facing pain and permitting yourself to feel the anger, the fear, the hurt, the grief, the sadness, and whatever else is in your heart. Rarely can this be accomplished alone. When reexperiencing memories of childhood abandonment, a person should not be left alone *again*. Being with others who are also opening their childhood hurts inspires, sometimes frightens, but always stimulates people to face their own resistance to pain. When you try to heal alone, you miss group energy and enthusiasm.

We call these temporary healing communities sacred circles whose power cannot be easily explained but only experienced. Within them, "little miracles" occur. One person will say what another finds especially meaningful. One person's work reminds another of a parent, or of a forgotten childhood incident.

STAGE 4

The Telling Works

As you tell your secrets, admitting how hurt and angry you feel, energy bound up in denial and repression is available to be expressed in assertiveness, playfulness, and joy. You take back your need to blame others and admit to your own feelings. As you express anger appropriately, you stop erupting at the people around you. You feel recognized for yourself. Positive feedback and small successes improve your self-esteem. You think of yourself as someone who "can do," instead of someone who can't. You explore new behavior and take chances. Life begins to change.

In a seminal book entitled *Self-Esteem,* Richard Bednar summarized years of research on this topic with this finding: People with self-esteem take personal responsibility and personal risks. Taking responsibility means you stop thinking of yourself as a victim and start to become the "lead" actor in your life's unfolding. Risk taking means taking on potentially rewarding opportunities even though they are difficult or might involve failure. It doesn't seem to matter whether the risks lead to disappointment. Such people use failures as learning opportunities and continue to like themselves.

As you confront your secrets, your shame continues to dissipate. You begin to reclaim your body and your sexual feelings. Pleasure becomes possible. You admit you are wounded, and believe you can heal. In this stage you are "working the program," telling the truth, confronting those you need to deal with, and learning to open up your feelings in healing ways.

In anonymous groups, in men's and women's gatherings, in therapy, anywhere that people gather to create sacred space for healing, you can unburden yourself. Within the sacred space, you learn new behavior through trial and error. Your defenses are lowered. You listen and give focused attention to others. You identify with others rather than distancing yourself.

Jim, a thirty-five-year-old computer programmer, is a dramatic example of "The Telling Works." Jim was angry and isolated when he entered this stage. He had few friends, and although he was unhappy and lonely, he didn't know he was grieving the loss of his childhood. Jim believed he was "basically a happy guy." He proved this to himself through frequent use of what he thought was a charming laugh. To everyone else it sounded like a discordant screech.

Jim took a five-day workshop with us. Three days into the workshop some members shared their reactions with Jim. Laurie told Jim that when he laughed she had no idea what he was really feeling, and it scared her. Pam said that when *she* giggled inappropriately she was often unaware that actually she felt sad or mad. Gretl told her childhood story, and Jim was struck by its similarity to his. When Gretl cried and he cried with her, Jim realized he should shed tears for himself. When Donald ripped a pillow apart expressing his rage at the father who beat him, Jim's clenched fists told him that he felt anger, too.

The next day Jim confessed that when he was nine years old, his mother locked herself and his sister in a bedroom and forced Jim to go downstairs and confront his drunken father, who had a knife. As he told this story, Jim talked in a flat voice, but we could tell he had enormous feelings about this abuse. Getting up from the chair where he sat, Jim clenched his fists, took a pillow and pummeled it until he was exhausted.

After Jim revealed his secret, his crazy laugh came out less often and eventually stopped altogether a few years later. Jim set out to learn to express himself more effectively, sharing what he really felt. People in the group drew close to him over the next two days. One of the older men became a mentor. And Jim, having for the first time people who cared about him, learned how to be real. After the workshop, Jim joined an ACOA group in his hometown and continued his healing. A year later he wrote to tell us that he had a girlfriend for the first time, and he was beginning to experience the payoff from all his work. Sharing his childhood secrets, although painful, freed him from hiding from life.

The Intention: The intention to heal is very strong in this stage. Exposing pain-avoidant mechanisms, including addictive behaviors, takes priority over making life-enhancing decisions. People in this stage sometimes forgo sexual relationships, because the priority is their emotional healing and because the risk of relapse at this level of excitement and stress is so great.

STAGE 5

Stuck in the Telling

Disclosing secrets, which in stages 3 and 4 is an important step in recovery, becomes a trap in stage 5. Here, you become a therapy or twelve-step junkie. You identify yourself as an "ACOA" or as an abuse survivor, and become stuck in self-disclosure. Confession follows confession, each one more horrific. You believe erroneously that if you just keep telling, life will work out.

In stage 5 you go from therapist to therapist seeking "the cure." Mistaking confessing for fun, your life is dominated by therapy and therapy groups. You believe sharing pain is the only meaningful way to know someone. Unsure of yourself, you substitute therapists and fellow self-helpers for intimate relationships.

Why are you telling all? Because you believe sharing your secrets enriches your life and the life of listeners. In addition, you are "addicted to excitement" as a way to deal with a deep-seated fear of being out of control. What in stages 3 and 4 is a way out of the shame becomes in stage 5 a habitual response that protects you from the unknown. After the secrets are told and the intense emotional work associated with those secrets has taken place, you must let go of being a victim and face life with an open heart. But when you are emotionally available for whatever life brings, you are very vulnerable. You may prefer painful memories because they are familiar. People who complain and habitually see the negative in everything feel secure because they believe they know what life is about. Nothing changes. Miserable as life is, it can be dealt with because it is certain. It is unimportant that your point of view brings little fulfillment or satisfaction.

Therapy and self-help groups are vital to recovery. Daily attendance in a group may be crucial for a period of time. In stage 3 or 4, sharing your secrets is extremely valuable. But eventually the secrets have been shared, the historically based pain expressed, and it is time to move on.

Letting go of the identity of a sufferer is scary. At that moment, nothing else takes its place. You must face the "void"—the vacuum between letting go of the known and waiting for what's next. Many cannot bear this tension, this waiting, this emptiness. They hold on to the image of themselves as wounded children, or as people who cannot be fulfilled or satisfied in life. Even more insidious, some people in this stage have a self-righteousness about them that reflects a contempt for others who choose not to open their pain on request.

What you avoid in stage 5 is your own uniqueness and essential aloneness in life. In stages 3 and 4, as you shared secrets, you discovered that you were not the only one who experienced or felt what you did. The isolation that estranged you from your own self needed to be broken down. Healing was found in the discovery of your commonality, your ordinariness. But after the sense of isolation is healed, there is then the brave step into the solitude of your particular life. This means that no matter how much you may share with others, you are born alone and you die alone. The path that you take is shaped by your unique responses to the events that occur in your life.

Ultimately, all the sharing or advice in the world cannot determine the decisions you make. You are responsible for your own choices, for your own self. The feeling of oneness you experience when you discover a secret in common, or when you witness the release of someone's deeply held pain, is a holy moment, a divine relief from the solitary burden of life. But to think that this can be a way of life avoids taking responsibility for your own destiny, your own aloneness.

Edith, forty-five, a recently divorced mother with a grown son, joined our group as part of a three-year odyssey to find herself. At that time, she had just learned about the concept of being an ACOA and wanted to ex-

plore its meaning for her. Because Edith had been traveling the country attending one group after another, she
was more experienced than anyone in our group at
working on herself. She also was the most difficult to understand. Edith's language was "therapeutized" to the
point that it was impossible to feel the truth of anything
she said. We had the impression that Edith had taken on
the composite viewpoint of every therapist she had ever
encountered.

On her first night, Edith spilled out her sad history. It
contained such lurid details that it seemed impossible
that she could feel safe enough to divulge this information so quickly. As the evening went on, she continually
interrupted group members to add to her story or tell us
about a "fabulous" workshop or some "wonderful train-
ing" she had received.

By the end of the evening, the group members felt
battered by Edith. No one approached her to say good
night. Edith had made being a "sufferer" into a way of
life. She had perfected a therapeutic personality. She of-
fended people with her eagerness to disclose every detail
about her life. It was time for her to move on to discover
who she was under the layers of "eager lay psychologist"
that had become a frigid mask over her real self.

The Intention: The healing process is so rich in emotion and cathartic awakening that people confuse the
mechanism with its message of vitality. Thus, the positive
intentions of stage 5 to continue to grow to greater emotional maturity are blocked by the intention to stay involved with the healing process itself. It is time, however,
to look outside yourself for ways to express your vitality
in all your relationships, not just your therapeutic ones.
This is similar to a comment by philosopher Alan Watts
on the repeated use of LSD to attain spiritual enlighten-

ment: "Once you get the message, hang up the phone." The healing process goes on throughout a person's life, but after a while, it also interferes with the pleasure of living a full life.

STAGE 6

Secrets to Tell, Secrets to Keep, and Knowing the Difference—Emotional Maturity

In stage 6, you make the huge step toward acceptance of your aloneness and your unique destiny. In fact, you find strength in your growing self-knowledge. You now begin to discriminate between secrets you need to tell to enhance the quality of your life and those you choose to contain so as to develop a stronger sense of self. You are no longer afraid or compelled to share your secrets; now, you operate out of free choice. The concept of reciprocity in self-disclosure takes over, so that when someone tells you about yesterday's ball game, you don't respond with a story about childhood abuse.

You view making contact and experiencing closeness with others as treasured events, but no longer a necessity for your sense of well-being. You create opportunities for these kinds of closeness as a matter of course in your life. You also value your time alone, and begin to connect deeply with an inner sense of knowing what is right for you. You do not look to others to help you feel good about yourself. Codependency is not active in this stage. Feeling unity with yourself becomes more important than feeling unity with anyone else. This may be a time of great sprifual growth, the development of what we call an internal sacred space.

At this stage, you are aware that your spouse or lover is separate from you. In fact, your differences create excitement. You begin to honor your uniqueness instead of trying to become "one" through sharing secrets or changing the other person's mind about something. You now know that relationships are for pleasure, not for working on your "stuff." You recognize the difference between secrets that harm and secrets that help. And you have the maturity and emotional sobriety to protect those you care about from indiscriminate sharing of what might be going on with them. You've learned about the importance of timing and appropriateness in your sharing. You are not afraid to make errors in your relationships because you see them as learning experiences. You find people and places to share your concerns in ways that will be life enhancing.

Recently, Emily, a lovely twenty-seven-year-old who worked with us for several years, moved into this stage. Her focus switched from being the client to being the therapist as she completed her master's in counseling. Emily found intense feelings exciting and had no trouble separating her own concerns from those of the group or of the clients. Emily's fiancé, Rick, who had a successful career in real estate, delighted in Emily's success and encouraged her. It was a pleasure for us to see how much they enjoyed each other's company, a marked shift from her last boyfriend, with whom almost every meeting involved some confrontation or fight, where he seemed threatened by her feelings and determined to be right about whatever opinion he held.

Emily enjoyed her life and did not hesitate to show this to others. Her past was not suppressed but a part of the fabric of her life. Her heart was present because she was not afraid of the grief and rage that occurred when she was reminded of her father's arrogance or her mother's capitulation to him. She trusted the healing process. She also trusted her sexuality. This meant she allowed herself erotic responses to men and women other than her fiancé, but kept them to herself and did not act out.

Emily decided not to tell Rick about the attraction that she felt toward a member of the staff at the clinic where she worked. She knew that she would never act on this desire, and her feelings didn't interfere with her love for Rick. She had developed into an emotionally sober young woman who was creating a powerful inner sanctum. She had discovered pleasure, fun, and the ability to share them with another person. Emily had learned to focus her life on healthy pleasures sustained by a confidence that she could face life's unfolding.

The Intention: Intention is simplified at this stage because it is guided by one's own tastes and preferences. A person knows how to pursue pleasure with a spirit of caring for others.

STAGE 7

Freedom

(Karen discovered this stage and then wrote this section in the last months of her life. This stage reflects Karen's acceptance of her own dying and the gratitude she felt for the richness of her life.)

Emotionally sober, willing to let go of past pain, this is the stage in which you no longer identify yourself as having been wounded or abused. You know that you are more than that. The sacred space you have created inside yourself connects you to what some call the divine will, where you know yourself to be more than this body or that particular set of experiences.

At this stage you are so aligned with your destiny that you take responsibility for what life holds for you, and you make conscious choices about what you want. If you are feeling tired and defeated, you recognize that it is of your own doing, and that it is *you* that you need to change. You accept life's unfolding as a natural flow that you respond to with confidence and self-respect. There is no blame in this stage. If you have created misery for yourself, you honor it as part of your learning, allow yourself to feel it, and let it go. You are sure about what you want and create it through clear intentions, using affirmations and other forms of positive thinking and visualization.

Often people skip to this step prematurely, confusing denial with letting go. If you are in pain, it does not work to assert: "I am happy, I am happy." Denying what exists does not change anything. But if you feel your pain completely, and then you can let it go, it eventually disappears from your consciousness. In place of the emptiness that is left, you create new intentions. As you focus your life on a positive intention, you have a clear shot at success. This phenomenon is analogous to a baseball player who has a high batting average of around .300. This means seven out of ten times he makes an out. Yet, he does not focus on his rate of failure; rather, he starts fresh at each opportunity at bat with the intention of complete success. He cultivates tunnel vision regarding his potential and his intention to fulfill it.

In this stage you can even learn how to control how you feel and discover that it is your divine right to feel ecstatic. Simply being emotionally sober is not enough. You recognize when you are projecting inner feelings onto people in your environment, and you can take care of it, without involving anyone else. The long confrontations you used to have to "work things out" are no longer necessary. You know, as many Eastern spiritual teachers say, it is "all your own dream."

You trust your intuition, and when there is a decision to be made, you consult your inner guide. You are not afraid any longer to be your own authority, and you are confident about the steps you take. When you share your feelings with others, it is because you choose to, not out of compulsion or need. Your relationships, though intimate enough to handle any problem you might bring to them, are based on pleasure. You share what feels life enhancing to you. Rather than thinking that your idiosyncrasies need fixing, you accept them as part of who you are. Whether you are someone who enjoys a lot of company or prefers to be alone, your sense of aliveness and deep inner peace is attractive to others.

The Intention: Achieving this stage may appear similar to the search for the Holy Grail or enlightenment in Buddhism—the focus is on the going, not on getting there.

In the next chapter we show you how to go forward with your own and others' secrets with the use of the Life Enhancement Grid. Knowing what stage you are in provides both guidance and compassion for your healing journey. Do not skip steps. It doesn't work and it blinds you to the task of learning by trial and error.

Healing Secrets

The next story captures the stages and phases of the healing process of two individuals. Stages are fluid phenomena, and people can be in different ones at the same time. You may be operating primarily in one stage and have a stressful situation throw you back to a place where you think of yourself as "in the soup" again. Don't be discouraged.

Christopher and Melanie's Story

Christopher, thirty-four, had used his charm to develop a multimillion dollar commercial real estate company. He was proud of his accomplishment. He had worked hard to keep his clients happy, and to protect his employees. Their benefit package was one of the best in the business. With the recent recession, however, his business slumped dramatically. Christopher's company couldn't withstand the crisis in investor confidence. Christopher was devastated, agonizing about his clients' losses and the employees he had to lay off. As time went on, he examined his own role in the failure. In his mind he was responsible. What did Christopher believe about life that caused him to crash so spectacularly?

By the time we met him, Christopher had decided he had been on the wrong track. His destiny, he was sure, was not simply to make money. He wanted to help heal others as well as solve the planet's environmental problems. First, however, he knew he had to heal himself. Following a friend's advice and suspecting that he had some dark secrets, he came to one of our workshops. He brought with him his fiancée, Melanie. She came because she loved him, not because she wanted to do her own emotional work. Both were in the "In the Soup" stage.

Melanie, cute and cheerful, believed in fairy tales. She wanted her relationship with Christopher to be perfect. Having no idea what to do with negative feelings, she simply erased them. Her childhood, she told us on opening night, was fine. As we later discovered, she came from an extremely private family whose secrets were very well kept.

The Exploration

For the first week, Christopher and Melanie mostly listened. As a "happy" couple, they were sometimes like fish in a fishbowl, with the other group members peering in. After several days, it became obvious even to them that they clung to their "family of two" to avoid the emotional cauldron that was boiling for everyone. They worked out a jealousy issue between them, sympathized with and supported other members of the group, but maintained that nothing in their lives was as serious as what other group members faced.

Then one day, when the workshop participants had divided into small groups, Christopher told Terry about a childhood incident. When he was thirteen, his mother took him to a hotel and taught him how to have sex. Afterwards, his mother told him she didn't have an orgasm, and Christopher felt he had failed her. From that time on, he had been terrified to displease any woman. Because he *had* had an orgasm, he did not think of himself as sexually abused. But as he confessed to Terry, he became aware of a lifetime pattern of compulsively trying to please women. "All my life," Christopher said, "I've been taking care of people, trying to make up for the fact that I had had sex with my mother and couldn't make her have an orgasm." But his guilt, he saw, made him fail in other parts of his life, also. "I couldn't let myself be a success, not with a crime like incest on my record."

The Catharsis

"Thank God that business collapsed," Christopher said. "I was wiping myself out taking on more and more people than I could be responsible for. I was exhausting myself."

Now that the secret was out, Christopher got to choose how he would continue to live his life. The first choice he confronted was whether or not to tell Melanie. Should he protect her or not? Did he need her to know? Terry advised him to go slowly, to live with the secret and feel in his body how it would be to share it with Melanie. Karen told Christopher that if she were he, she'd tell. A few days later, when they were feeling particularly close while eating dinner, Christopher told Melanie. She threw up into her napkin. Poor Christopher was convinced that he disgusted her.

Later, at our workshop, Melanie expressed her feelings. "I'm not disgusted with you, Christopher. It's your *mother* who is disgusting," said Melanie. She put her arms around Christopher and he broke into great wrenching sobs. After a few hours he became furious. With the men standing around him, he built a tower of pillows which he then pummeled, screaming at his mother for abusing him, at his father for encouraging his mother to do this to him "so that [he] could justify sexually abusing my sisters," and at both of them for being so crazy. Finally spent, lying in Melanie's arms, he confessed, "Melanie told me that I made love mechanically. I didn't know what she meant, but now I see. I've been a robot all my life."

Several days later Melanie entered an exploration phase of her own by telling us about her childhood home where her father held them captive with his rage.

"I was so terrified," she said, tears rolling down her cheeks, "that I just got sweeter and sweeter, hoping I would never attract his anger. I don't just want to be nice, I want to be *real*." Being real for Melanie meant exploring the rage she knew was inside. Eventually she was able to express some of it to a man who enrolled as her father for a psychodramatic event.

Individuation

With the facing of their secrets, Melanie and Christopher were beginning to heal and were creating the foundation for a solid and supportive relationship. They needed, however, to begin with reality. Fairy tales do not endure. After the catharsis, they were open to having more contact with other group members. They did not have images to live up to anymore. Using the Life Enhancement Grid described in the next chapter, they chose to not confront their parents. Christopher's mother had desperately apologized for her reprehensible behavior within days of the event. This, however, only increased his sense of obligation to her because he tried to reassure her that "it wasn't so bad." Now, he didn't see the benefit of bringing it up again to an already unhappy old woman. Melanie felt sure that discussion of her childhood would be perceived as disrespectful and be disregarded by both of her parents.

The healing process involves going through these cycles repeatedly because it is not just an intellectual endeavor. Christopher and Melanie, for example, had to face and feel the pain of their abuse repeatedly, as well as take personal responsibility for the years of personal suffering they caused themselves by their adult decisions to hide from it. As they recovered the memories intellectually, they also discovered that they would have a bodily "felt memory" of the experiences, a phrase developed by Eugene Gendlin in his book, *Focusing*. Usually people can come up with a word or phrase that captures such experiences in childlike terms as they explore the past by focusing on the body responses to the memory. For example, Christopher's phrase for this experience was "This is horrible."

In therapy, clients often have a cognitive realization of a past event. But if awareness does not include expressing the depth of the feeling related to the event, then the denial in the psyche is not completely released. Without feeling the feelings, you quickly return to "it was not so bad" and to skepticism. To let go of a past pain, the very issues of the body have to release it. This cannot happen in the absence of feeling. Most often, catharsis includes some sort of crying, shaking, yelling, and raging, although sometimes the release can be as soft as a whisper. However it occurs, it has to happen in the body.

Christopher and Melanie had a long way to go in their healing journey, but the introduction to emotional healing just described here gave them enough access to their emotional life to allow them to begin using the Life Enhancement Grid to handle their secrets. This instrument is described in the next chapter.

5

The Life Enhancement Grid

*"I don't want to tell my wife everything, nor do I
want to hear all her secrets. Recently she went on
a river-rafting trip by herself. I am sure there were
little flirtations and that was part of the fun for
her. But I don't want to hear about it. Nor do I
want to tell her everything that I think or
everything that I do. A feeling of privacy is very
important to me, and I like having a part of my
life that only I know about."*

—VICTOR

After a number of years of marriage Victor and
Anna discovered that some secrecy and privacy deepened the mystery between them.
This, in turn, heightened the sexual bond. When Victor
and Anna first met, like many couples, they felt an overwhelming "urge to merge" and confess all. They were
best friends and soul mates, and were thrilled by their
similarities. After a while, they found themselves wanting
more individual privacy. Because they were mature and
had attained a degree of emotional sobriety, they established a distance and a closeness that felt just right to
them. As a result, their sexual attraction remains high.

They are very excited by each other, and very much in love.

ANNA: "We had to learn that being therapists to each other didn't help our sexuality. It was tough for us, for I am a psychotherapist and Victor is a kind and loving physician. Our first instincts were to nurture each other and help each other understand our deepest concerns. But we got lost in a kind of sticky enmeshment, and pretty soon we weren't making love anymore. So we stopped 'confessing' to each other. We still can serve as sounding boards for one another, and Victor is often the first person I turn to when I am really upset, but I do my therapy elsewhere."

Neither Victor nor Anna depends on the other for a sense of fulfillment or self-esteem. Within their private core, they have a sense of self separate from their relationship and from each other. They are together for the pleasure of each other's company, not to work on "issues" or "resolve buried feelings." Pleasure between them is based on the sexual bond. How did they learn which secrets to tell and which to keep? How did they learn to be honest with each other while retaining a private place? How do they keep the mystery and excitement alive? These are the questions we answer in this chapter.

Mystery in the Voyeuristic Society

The voyeuristic society sacrifices vitality, excitement, and mystery for the false security and control that comes from knowing as much about a subject as possible. This is particularly true for people from dysfunctional homes where power was abused, or where the marital difficulties led to suffering for the entire family.

By contrast, in healthy families, children learn autonomy slowly as their personal boundaries develop within the confines of familiar relationships. Over time, children create a strong sense of self, understanding what is proper and timely self-disclosure. Healthy children admit misdeeds. They also keep personal diaries, close doors, have private thoughts, and share intimate conversations.

As you shall see, the Life Enhancement Grid helps explore the problem of balancing intimacy and privacy so that a person's sense of autonomy is supported. To use the grid, however, one must have a strong sense of separateness, the very sensibility undermined by the voyeuristic society.

Revaluing Modesty and Self-Consciousness

To rediscover personal privacy and develop an inner sense of self, we encourage our clients to honor their own shyness and modesty—that their inner life has a personal worth that is not for everyone's eyes. Shyness and modesty develop when children become fully conscious of their separateness from others. Their personal boundaries are fragile, and self-expression is very important to them. They need patient, focused attention to be comfortable with their feelings.

Drawing personal boundaries requires healthy self-consciousness that, at its extreme, can cause someone to be paralyzed with shyness. People also need sufficient vitality to define themselves, and the maturity to accept human limitations. Healthy people are tentative. They don't barge into others' lives, but carefully explore the possibilities of a relationship. Compulsive and exhibitionist truth-telling has little to do with intimacy and a lot to do with craving attention. Inevitably, this craving is met with rejection because other adults won't deal with the neediness. The person who craves attention withdraws into a shell, feeling shame and believing that intimacy is impossible.

Healthy and Unhealthy Privacy Defined

Healthy privacy is very different from the withdrawal into hopelessness just described. Privacy means that some thing or some idea belongs to a particular person or group. The holder of secrets believes that disclosure leads to suffering for someone. Privacy is necessary to discover the depths of a being's personality and soul. A person needs to be by and with himself or herself to do that. Thoughts need to be distilled slowly before being made ready for public consumption. Having a sense of privacy denotes a maturity that is missing when one is too "open," causing conflict, or too "closed," causing shame. Privacy is at the core of an individual's self-esteem.

Unhealthy privacy, on the other hand, is treacherous. It excludes others from information needed to reveal the truth. Unhealthy privacy usually involves a misuse of power. Often, holders of secrets justify their behavior without carefully considering the situation. "It's for your own good" is a rationale used to control others.

Privacy must also be defined specifically for different relationships: marital and sexual, collegial, mentor, friendship (same or opposite gender), and parental. Each have different characteristics.

Marital and Sexual Privacy

These relationships operate in such a way that appropriate revelation varies greatly, depending on the moment. At one point, a person may feel so close to another person that all secrets can be revealed; at other times, he or she believes the relationship is enhanced through mystery and curiosity. Unfortunately, many couples define intimacy in general and sexual intimacy in particular as being associated with full disclosure no matter what the cost.

Collegial and Professional Privacy

This is tricky. Competitive and cooperative values flourish simultaneously. Small self-disclosures create warmth that enhances cooperation. Often, however, colleagues compete for a promotion or scarce resources, which can cause both parties to feel threatened about sharing information.

Some studies have indicated that productivity is enhanced by personal self-disclosure, especially where cooperation and high-level skills are required. Other studies show the opposite, especially when the job is repetitive or discipline is necessary. Self-disclosure of intimate details can cloud judgment as people second-guess the motivation behind the disclosure.

We would argue strongly that the sharing of secrets be carefully considered using the Life Enhancement Grid. Damage control on the job is very difficult. A confidant today can be a source of job stress tomorrow.

Mentor Privacy

These relationships must be open to be useful. Most successful individuals we know, including ourselves, have found that using someone older to lean on is of critical importance in learning a profession and in planning long-term actions. Confidentiality must be assured before entering into such a relationship. The best mentors are older and have already achieved the goals you are seeking. They articulate the secrets of achieving those goals and have a genuine desire to see you succeed.

Same-Gender Friend Privacy

Perhaps this is the richest territory for intimacy because of the opportunity for deep empathy. Men and women *do* have different experiences; however, men infrequently take advantage of their friendships. Instead, they let competitiveness and fear of being vulnerable, as well as homophobia, block expressions of warmth and enthusiasm. Men, in our experience, rarely share personal concerns or solicit help.

Opposite-Gender Friend Privacy

These are treasured relationships. Once it is understood that sexual feelings will not be acted on, important concerns are addressed through what family therapist David Kantor calls "gender conversation." These talks assume we can enjoy and learn if we can agree to differ, rather than be blinded by the perspective of gender or insist on a "correct" way of seeing a situation.

Parental Privacy

Parents have always had secrets from their children that are important to keep because of children's vulnerability. Children need to have secrets, too, because it deepens their sense of self. Having a secret hiding place or a special language with a friend enables a child to trust his or her own autonomy.

The Life Enhancement Grid

You should now have a firm understanding of what we consider to be privacy and its limits. It is time to learn how to make choices about what information to share and what to withhold. Over the past several years, we have developed a method that helps our clients decide which secrets to tell and which to keep. We call this the Life Enhancement Grid. This tool, which on the surface may look simplistic, reveals profound insights. The grid includes the following quadrants:

	Is life enhancing to me	Is not life enhancing to me
Is life enhancing to the other	TELL	TELL
Is not life enhancing to the other	TELL SOMEONE ELSE	DON'T TELL

As you can see, when telling a secret is life-enhancing to both you and another, the secret should be told. Even when telling a secret is *not* life enhancing to you, but is to another person, you should tell. However, when the reverse occurs—it's life enhancing to you, not to the other—then you should tell, but the telling should be with someone other than the person for whom it would have a negative effect. Finally, when a secret does not enhance either party, it should not be told.

When we talk of life enhancement, we enter into an intellectual minefield. Often our minds know, but we have so many contradictory thoughts that we can't tell whether or not a certain action or self-disclosure is life enhancing. The body, however, always knows.

The Body as Guide—Using the Body Scan to Assess Life Enhancement

The body is a living organism, a rich resource of feedback and intuition. It is not about "reasoning." It communicates with the ego through feeling. When people feel something "in their bones" or "in their guts," a certainty exists that supports even high-risk undertakings. You know what is right for you.

Unfortunately, traumatized people are pain- and pleasure-avoidant. For them, body messages do not get through. In such people, physical cues are so separated from emotional cues that two different kinds of feeling exist: physical feelings (hurt, taste, touch) and emotional feelings (joy, sorrow, anger, fear).

Besides this separation based on abuse, two other factors cause this split. One is that "feelings" get divided early in life because schools emphasize being rational rather than intuitive or emotional. The second factor is that adults are threatened by the vitality of children, who are most visible in their aggression and sensuality. Adults often unconsciously and against their own better judgment desire to suppress children in their playfulness, tireless excitement, sense of wonder, and even in their capacity to love unconditionally. Parents deaden children's vitality through criticism, overt shaming, or simply ignoring them.

The ability to assess what is life enhancing is directly related to your capacity to attend to the body and its feelings. Unless it is sufficiently vital, body feedback may be hard for you to receive. However, we use a method with our clients called the Body Scan, which enables people to understand their body's language and use it as a trusted consultant.

Here is how it works:

1. *Quieting Yourself:* The first step is to quiet yourself enough to observe what is going on inside the body. Any meditation technique will do. If you have no experience, close your eyes and attend to your breathing as if you are watching it from a distance. Then, disconnect from your thoughts by simply noticing when a thought or other distraction grabs your attention. Gently and without criticism withdraw your attention from the thought and bring it back to your breath. Are you breathing deeply, with equal inhalation and exhalation?

2. *Scanning Your Body:* Once you have quieted yourself, relax your focus from the breath alone to an awareness of your entire body. Scan your body, noticing tension where it exists. As you do this, continue to be aware of your breathing. Is your diaphragm relaxed? How are your abdominal muscles? The back of your neck? Do you have a headache? Does your heart hurt? Pain, tension, and contraction signal discomfort. A relaxed, full-breathing body indicates that all is well.

Some people live with so much body tension that this feedback causes distress. This is a signal that something is disturbing and not life enhancing. Initially fear may override any risks you might consciously consider taking; however, with experience, risk taking becomes exciting. Life-enhancing choices are often uncomfortable, but you make them because they are right for you and for the person you are sharing your secrets with.

3. *Using the Mind:* When you must decide whether revealing a secret would be life enhancing or not, use your mind. Ask yourself, would revealing this secret clarify, confuse, or burden you or another person? Then, sit quietly and focus on your body and your breathing. Imagine continuing to keep the secret. Notice how you feel. Now, imagine telling the secret, and again tune into your physical state. Does telling the secret:

- Release tension?
- Block energy?
- Create pleasure?
- Relieve pain?

4. *Scanning into the Future:* When tuning into your body, you need to project yourself into the future—into the time when the secret is already revealed (or continues to be concealed). Otherwise, you can get confused. In other words, it may be life enhancing for you to have your mother know that your stepfather assaulted you sexually, but the idea of informing her frightened you so that your diaphragm tensed up, your stomach knotted, and you couldn't breathe. This is a natural response to revealing upsetting information. If you imagine that you have told your mother and she knows, your breathing and muscles may relax, and calmness may replace fear. Practice leads to awareness of the patterns of your response and how to become comfortable with your choices.

With the body scan technique in mind, let's see in detail how the Life Enhancement Grid and body scanning works.

Three years ago, forty-five-year-old Rene became so depressed he attempted to drive his car off a steep mountain with his wife Joan beside him. The car hit a patch of ice and spun around several times, coming to a stop in the middle of the road. Rene never told Joan of his suicidal mission, but in our workshop he wondered if he should.

To help Rene decide if it would be life enhancing to reveal his secret, we took him through the following steps:

1. We asked him what it was like to have this secret. (Rene's eyes closed as he listened to his inner cues.)

RENE: "I carry it like a physical weight in my belly. I don't breathe deeply or fully—I have a constant feeling of not having enough air. The secret is often on my mind. I don't want to get close to Joan because I feel guilty."

Rene's shoulders appeared tense, and he carried them high. His face muscles were also tense, creating a pained and worried look. His back was hunched. He clearly was a burdened man. We pointed out these things to him.

2. We then asked him to imagine that Joan knew he tried to kill them both. What did it feel like?

RENE: "There is a barrier between us. I still think of it when I'm with her, but now I'm wondering what *she* is thinking. I still can't breathe."

3. Next, we asked him to project himself onto his wife, to *imagine* that he was she, and to notice how *her* *body* felt. With the secret still concealed, Rene described his wife's feelings.

RENE: "There's pain in her chest, she feels sad, she's confused about what is going wrong in our relationship. She knows I'm not with her, but she doesn't know why. She's trying to pretend everything is okay."

Projecting yourself onto another's reality is a leap of faith. You act as if it were true that you can do it, and using your imagination, you find that you can get an astounding amount of information.

4. Now, we said to Rene, imagine you had told Joan, how does she feel? Rene gasped with shock, and started holding his breath for long moments between inhales.

RENE: "My diaphragm hurts and I feel dizzy, scared, confused. If I tell Joan, I feel an important part of her will leave me completely. Her body is here, but most of her is running from me. She is terrified."

5. Finally, we asked Rene to tune into himself again, imagining that he had told his secret. His breathing was shallow, his shoulders raised in fear, but now his forehead hurt as he watched Joan constantly, scared that she no longer trusted him. He feared she would leave him. Clearly, telling his secret was not life enhancing to either of them. But neither was keeping it. What was he to do?

As we explored this dilemma with Rene week after week, we discovered that the depression that led to the suicide attempt was gone. Rene had entered therapy immediately after the suicide attempt and he felt he understood what had created his despair. He had worked through much of the rage that he had buried with the depression. He was, however, deeply ashamed and sorry for having risked his and Joan's life. He yearned for absolution. Rene had thought that if he confessed, Joan would forgive him, relieving him of the shame he carried. He now saw, however, that telling his secret would not enhance either of their lives, but would make them worse. Since what he needed was forgiveness, he had to forgive himself no matter how long it took.

As we worked with him, Rene felt inklings of compassion for himself. He recognized that suicide was the only solution he could think of to relieve his suffering at that time. He promised never to endanger his wife again, but to protect and care for her. After his resolution, he tuned into his body. Rene had made a life-enhancing decision. He was finally on a road that would lead to peace with himself.

Confession is tempting because the person doesn't have to bear the guilt of a past misdeed, particularly where infidelity is concerned or where distrust is no longer warranted. Such confession, we believe, is a mistake. Sexual jealousy has an energy and intensity that goes far beyond reason. Your partner may never forget. Thus, it is critical to consider what the other person will do with this information.

How to Tell a Secret Constructively

If you decide that you have a secret that should not be contained, how can you tell it constructively? Here are some ideas to consider:

  • Choose wisely whom you tell. Never pick someone who will be too upset, who won't believe you, or who will judge you harshly. A rehearsal with a friend, a sponsor, or a therapist is usually a good first step.

• Be aware of your motivation. What is it you want from the telling? Do you want advice? Support? Tell the listener ahead of time.

• Think of the effect on the person you are telling. Is it an unfair burden? Can he or she handle it? Assessing the maturity of a listener is a serious task.

• Be careful about when and where you tell the secret. Make sure there is time and privacy to deal with such powerful feelings as anger, shame, or sadness.

• Make the secret digestible. Tell it in stages. Be careful how you tell it, what elements you tell first, and what follows what.

• If aspects of the secret are frightening, you may want to reassure listeners—as in: "Everyone is going to be fine, but I want you to know that your family was in an accident today."

• Get the person's permission to tell the secret. Not everyone wants the burdens of other people's secrets.

• Create clear terms of confidentiality. Can the person tell her or his partner? No one? Is the person willing to receive the secret given those terms?

• Prepare the person you are telling by reassuring him or her of the outcome before you begin, such as: "It's all over, and I want to be with you, but I need you to know that Caroline and I slept together and she is going to call you about it." Or by warning the person of what you think his or her feelings may be, such as: "I don't want you to be frightened, but the bank is conducting an investigation of my accounts. It is going to be hard because I did some things that the bank may see as shifty, but my lawyer thinks I have a good case for acquittal."

• Be aware that you have known about this secret for a long time and have had a chance to understand your feelings about it. The person you are telling hasn't, so give her or him room to react emotionally. Sometimes this is hard. Having a third party present can be helpful. Ultimately, everything will be okay if it is fully discussed and the emotions fully felt. This, however, takes time and a strong measure of maturity.

With all this in mind, let's explore in depth the Life Enhancement Grid.

Telling Someone

We start with the quadrant where it is life enhancing to tell someone like a therapist or an anonymous fellowship.

Rene's story could have had a tragic ending if he had told his wife and she had reacted with the horror his secret warrants. If she had not trusted the healing that had since taken place, it could have become a disaster. But the weight of carrying that secret by himself was crushing Rene. He needed a safe place to go through his anguish and self-hatred without anyone else also going through it reacting negatively to him.

Sometimes talking to our parents directly results in eliciting apologies and reconciliation. But often parents are either dead or unwilling to express regret, particularly if their crimes were heinous or repressed through alcoholic blackouts. Many times, raising family secrets worsens relations and does not lead to healing.

This was true in the case of Janice, a forty-year-old woman who started having incest memories after her daughter was born. Her accusation of sexual fondling by her father led to estrangement from her entire family, including Janice's sisters, who had no such recollection. Janice's loneliness was a high price to pay when her own memories were so fuzzy.

Janice's family believed that she had been encouraged to make these accusations by the huge numbers of incest survivors coming forward publicly. The family saw her charges as her latest attempt to get attention. Janice was not prepared for her family's response, especially her sisters', with whom she had been close.

But to us, the important point is not whether these incest memories were accurate. Janice's memories were real to her and had to be worked through if she was to become sexually whole. She had to assume the memories were true to do this. The real question here was whether she served her healing by telling her family. We think *not*. She created a situation in which everyone thought she had distorted reality. She may spend the rest of her life trying to prove she hadn't. If she had dealt with her injury in sacred space, Janice could have focused on her healing, taking responsibility for its effect on herself, her husband, and her children. The "here and now" is much more important than exacting vengeance, punishment, or an apology.

Arthur discovered an equally destructive secret in therapy with us: his parents really didn't like him much, preferring his brother George. They saw Arthur's passive nature as an unsolvable problem. Arthur knew he had anxiety and low self-esteem when he came to see us, but he had never doubted his parents' love for him.

ARTHUR: "My parents wished they could love me more. They just don't like me the way I am. My brother George is much more assertive. We all think he is obnoxious sometimes, but I'm sure my parents are more comfortable with George's style than with mine. They complain to me about my choices and regularly communicate to me in subtle ways that I disappoint them. I know they don't mean to do this and they would be shocked that this is the way I see it. Again and again, I kept being made to feel like a loser in a family of winners. I used to say to myself, If only I'd tried harder. I now realize that this is useless. They are not bad people and they do love me in the way that they can. I feel so much relief knowing that their rejection of me was not something I could fix. I like myself now and don't apologize to them or to anyone."

Arthur made the right choice not to talk to his parents. They had done the best they could. Arthur paid the price until he worked it out for himself.

Telling Helps Another but Costs You

Telling a secret that makes another person's life better is a matter of integrity. Through experimentation we learn there is mutuality in most relationships. Looking out for your friend's best interest, even if it costs you, works. The price of not doing this, when it comes to secrets, is shame and guilt.

Shame is caused by trying to live up to an image of yourself that may be "attractive" to the rest of the world but is not you. Shame always feels intolerable and leads to lies and secrets. You let go of the "stuckness" that shame causes when you tell another your faults. This deepens intimacy. But *you* must bring your own guard down. Since people with shame feel that they have no real right to exist, they cope by trying to live up to an unreal image of themselves.

Let's look at some examples. Ed, a twenty-five-year-old electronics engineer, habitually deceived himself about how much time tasks would take. This naturally led to broken promises to friends and to his lover. Ed would become resentful as he overextended himself, lashing out at the people he cared about the most. When pushed by us to admit his responsibility for these repeated fiascoes, Ed turned beet red and replied, "I couldn't help it. If they only didn't expect so much of me." He stopped midsentence, seeing himself shift from responsibility to blame. Shame of failure was so great nothing else mattered to him. It was either-or for Ed; he was either the "big man" or the "foolish little boy." What he learned was that everyone around him saw right through his image as a big man. Eventually, Ed realized he could take on a lot less and still be appreciated.

Sandra and Jack came to couples therapy with a problem that clearly reflected gender differences: Sandra was very self-disclosing and wanted the same from her husband. Jack thought things were fine and only went to us to keep peace in the family. At a pivotal point in our sessions, Sandra asserted that intimacy meant that her feelings should be as important to Jack as they were to her. She was startled and angered when told by us that this was impossible.

Terry made this comment to Sandra: "I know your feelings are important to you and I respect that, but I find no reason why they should in any way be important to me. They are your feelings. I will listen and be interested in what you might feel or want from me, but I will insist on my right and responsibility to make up my own mind about what is important and to rely on my own thoughts and feelings rather than yours."

After she recovered from Terry's comments, Sandra

understood that her highly critical parents had assumed the right to decide what was important throughout her childhood. Sandra had naturally rebelled. She was surprised she had become the critical parent with Jack. Admitting that she wanted to be the focus of the couple caused embarrassment, but it allowed Jack to disclose his preferences for their relationship, something Sandra had wanted all along.

Disarming yourself and admitting your secret faults enhances other people's lives. It takes courage. It hurts. But the reward is intimacy and, often, reciprocal disclosures from others.

When Telling Enhances Life for Everyone

This quadrant is the easy one because it assumes the "truth will set you free." However, believing that telling what is true for you will make your life better is easier said than done because there is often an enormous inhibition to speaking out.

Willa and Hans were in trouble with their eight-month-old relationship when Willa came to us. Hans sometimes refused Willa's initiatives for making love. The rejections devastated Willa. She tried to be understanding, but her anger came out in enigmatic moodiness. When Hans asked her what she wanted, Willa could not say, even when she knew exactly what she wanted. This was especially true regarding sex, which was becoming increasingly unsatisfying for her. Willa believed that if she talked about her desires she would be seen as a "slut" and a "bitch" who was not "marriage material." For his part, Hans thought he was a great lover who didn't need to talk things over. It was hard giving up this belief, but it was much easier when he didn't have to read Willa's mind. After a while, they learned to talk about their preferences with a sense of humor.

An even harder life-enhancing self-disclosure is the one that is made when two people should not be together. Emily had wanted to break up with Lionel almost from the beginning of their relationship because he was so depressed and dependent on her. But she thought leaving Lionel was too cruel. Besides that, Emily was terribly afraid of being alone and had never broken up with anyone. Lionel was at least a safe harbor. Instead of talking about her rejection of Lionel, she would portray herself as being unable to get close to another person. Lionel would then insist that Emily had not given the relationship a chance. In turn, Emily would renew her efforts to make the relationship work. This is the same as believing your own press release because you read about it in the paper, even though you yourself gave out false information in the first place. This relationship dragged on for years in this way until it reached the inevitable conclusion of parting.

Telling No One

This quadrant becomes most useful as a person matures into a self-supporting autonomous adult. Keeping your awareness and inspirations to yourself is very empowering. As explained earlier, the danger of keeping things to yourself is that it eats away at your vitality. At some point, however, you know you can bare your own truth, however painful. Telling no one is right when retelling secrets adds to the psychic debris, and distracts from healing purposes. A good example comes from our own experience.

Terry and his wife, Gale, flew from Boston to California several years ago with their two children, Evan, then age four, and Avery, age two. It was a stressful situation because Avery was not feeling well. Both parents wanted to read and snooze. A short time into the flight, the plane began to bump on the jet stream currents. Gale reacted by hitting Terry on the head with a magazine to ensure he was being attentive to Avery.

TERRY: "I immediately felt insulted, believing that I was caring for the child and that Gale's way of getting my attention was infantalizing. I was enraged because I perceived her to have criticized me in a manner that humiliated me. I wanted to lash out, but kept my cool, instead saying, 'Do not hit me. There are other ways of getting my attention.' "

After a brief argument in which Gale justified her behavior and Terry defended his parenting skills, a half hour of quiet ensued. Terry used that time to probe his longing for female approval and his infantile rage that it was not always immediately available. Gale faced up to her self-righteousness, which masked a heartbreak labeled in her own therapy as, "a man will never be there for me." Terry and Gale apologized the next time they looked into each other's eyes.

The incident passed because they kept this internal processing to themselves. Was there a right or wrong here? We think not. Despite twenty years of revision of family roles brought on by the women's movement, mothers, in general, and Gale, in particular, are consistently more aware and responsive to their offspring than are most fathers. Does that give Gale the right to act without regard to Terry's personal boundaries? No. Does Gale's boundary violation give Terry the right to rage at controlling women? Of course not. No relationship thrives when rage is acted out repeatedly. Many couples struggle with the results of rage. Many even glamorize how openly violent they are with each other. In our experience, the price of having to heal the wounds of being raged at by a loved one is too high.

One of the great paradoxes of the current culture is that most people act quietly all day long at work, often enduring verbal assaults and humiliation with equanimity. When they return home, however, they let the slightest irritations become grounds for a fight. The apparent premise is that if we love each other, we have to put up with each other's crankiest self-expressions. This is not healthy. Consider the opposite premise: "This relationship is so precious to me that I will care for it like fine china. I will treat our time together as a special occasion."

Telling no one secrets that are yesterday's news and that may turn a relationship into a psychological melodrama is ultimately about healthy privacy. When your claim to privacy is full of shame, it is supported by fear of greater suffering and humiliation. Healthy privacy empowers you as you feel responsible for your inner life and consciously make choices. Of course, you can never be absolutely certain of your life-enhancement conclusions. You can only do the best you can.

Taking a risk reflects self-esteem and the development of integrity. The secrets people encounter in themselves and others are opportunities for deepened intimacy, even when the decision is to not share. Intimacy is not simply closeness and complete disclosure. That is the voyeuristic definition. Rather, it is the ability to be fully truthful with yourself and another even when that means keeping something to yourself.

For the best use of the Life Enhancement Grid, we

teach our clients that they must understand that secrets are gifts and that they involve notions of respect and integrity.

Secrets as Gifts

With a focus on positive, life-enhancing choices, your perspective on secrets changes dramatically, for intimacy is defined not only by what you share but also by what you hold private. You become more honest with yourself when you share your secrets. They are gifts, designed to enhance the life of another. Intimacy involves wanting the listener to know you better, whether or not the self-disclosure is painful.

With healthy personal boundaries, others are invited into your inner sanctum. They are honored guests and know it. Therapeutic environments support this inner sanctum, and healthy use of them sustains inner life. The line between what and when to disclose or not remains subtle and personal in healthy people. Your mystery is unspoken and serves as a magnet to others' interest and curiosity. Their desire to know you as an equal is engaged. The relationship is based on healthy excitement about what you will reveal to them about yourself.

We do the work of emotional healing so that our clients know deep in their bones that their friend or lover is not making them feel mad, sad, scared, or even happy. We are already full of these feelings and what we choose to share of ourselves is part of our personal mystery. Events and people activate our feelings. When clients accept their independence from others, they have more choice about whether to let themselves get swept up in a personal drama with full self-disclosure or simply keep their response to themselves. Feelings are precious gems not to be squandered on people who don't respect them.

Respect

Respect implies a genuine consideration of what is best for everyone concerned with a situation—yourself, others, and even the circumstance in which an exchange takes place (e.g., not a supermarket checkout line). When you have respect, you want everyone to win, if possible. Respect requires paying attention and carefully observing input from the environment and from the individuals in it. Respect means accepting the limitations and personal boundaries others have established.

Life enhancement requires a well-developed ability to see the world from other people's point of view. You learn there is no one right answer in any given situation. Even our preferences evolve in a dialogue where one person is free to disagree without losing the other person's respect.

Respect does not come because we want to give it or receive it. Respect occurs the old-fashioned way, you earn it. This happens by being honest about yourself and your preferences. You also earn it by demonstrating to yourself and others that you take responsibility for your actions and your fate. By fate, we refer to the events that happen to you and have happened to you in the past. Your fate is not necessarily your future.

TERRY: "I joined a men's group several years ago and have witnessed the blooming of mutual respect. Initially, at least for me, what I might have called respect was fear—that I was not as cool, as articulate, or as accomplished as the others. I grew up in a very competitive home and often found myself imagining competition when there was none. The men's group instead offered focused attention when a member talked of his heart's concerns. There is no leader. Personal stories often revolved around telling secrets. The meetings became filled with memories and feelings. I have developed a sense of awe for each person's ability to live his life with careful consideration and courage. I didn't always agree with some of the members' choices, but knowing their way of doing things deepened my respect for them.

"The interest and respect we offer each other creates an environment where tough choices can be thought through with feeling. Successes and failures are shared. The men's group was one of the first places where someone else's success brought unmitigated joy to me, rather than a nagging and almost unconscious sense that I have lost something by not keeping up."

Respect is earned when a person tells a secret at a time, in a place, and in a manner that is life enhancing for all present.

Integrity

We define integrity as behavior in which no action or feeling is inconsistent with a person's values. Most important, a person with integrity does not have trouble when his heart pushes him one way and his head the other. He knows himself. When a person has integrity, he is also not afraid to say

- "I don't know."
- "I made a mistake."
- "I need help."
- "I'm sorry."

By knowing your goals and values, you can make consistent choices and take action. Without integrity, life-enhancement decisions for yourself or for others are difficult. We all have many moments of stress during which we might be tempted to look to others to validate our self-worth and define our preferences and responsibilities. This impulse, however, is simply self-destructive. To use the Life Enhancement Grid effectively, you cannot act this way.

For example, Jack, an extremely bright, single, forty-seven-year-old management consultant, attended our workshop with a great deal of excitement. After years of "talking" therapy which had "gotten [him] nowhere," he became enthusiastically involved in emotional healing. Before long, however, Jack directed his anger at us. He was discouraged that results were not immediate.

Jack had been a victim in his childhood. His father was arrogant and abusive, while his mother stood by, justifying her passivity as marital duty. For Jack to develop integrity, he would have to work through his rage because it was directed at anyone who came close. With adulthood, however, comes responsibility for one's anger. Jack had trouble accepting this because it was painful and humiliating. He didn't like that he consistently became angry. Isolating himself was a life-enhancing choice because Jack lacked sufficient integrity to admit that he didn't know how to get close to someone.

Janice, a thirty-two-year-old dental hygienist, came to our workshop with the opposite problem, but she also lacked integrity. Married to a handsome and successful physician, she had it all, at least by outward appearance. Janice, however, did not love her husband, Bert. She did not like the way Bert controlled her, but she never told him she preferred anything else. The safety of her marriage took priority. She had never lived by herself, or made decisions without first considering the impact on others. Janice's marriage had withered and died because no one ever encouraged her to have an independent identity, let alone integrity.

Would it have been useful for Janice to take the risk of sharing her feelings with Bert before it came to this point? Of course. But she was so full of fears that she could not make life-enhancing choices. Careful and deep emotional work helped Janice find herself so she could make her own choices. Perhaps if Bert had done the same, the marriage could have been saved. But he had chosen a woman without apparent integrity, who had been willing to be a doormat for him. This was what Bert believed he wanted in a wife. Perhaps this was what he was familiar with at home when he grew up and at the hospital where nurses defer to his wishes because he's a doctor. When Janice spoke up, he considered her a "feminist bitch" and wanted out of the marriage.

Janice and Bert's story highlights another point. As Janice developed into a woman with integrity and respect, she lost her marriage. Very often personal growth upsets the status quo. It takes courage to move forward in life and to accept the consequences of your actions. Like the Life Enhancement Grid, life itself is a learning process.

Now that you more fully understand the Life Enhancement Grid, the body scan technique, and our notions about which secrets to tell and which to keep, we can examine the variety of secrets people hold. We begin with generational secrets.

6

Generational Secrets

*In an old house there is always listening,
and more is heard than is spoken.
And what is spoken remains in the room,
waiting for the future to hear it.
And whatever happens began in the past,
and presses hard on the future.
The agony in the curtained bedroom,
whether of birth or of dying,
Gathers into itself all the voices of the past,
and projects them into the future.*

T. S. ELIOT, *THE FAMILY REUNION*

In this chapter we explore the impact of generational secrets kept by a family to "protect" their children. We call these generational secrets because they concern events in a family's life that occur *before* the birth of children, as opposed to family secrets that happened *during* the children's lifetimes. (At the end of this chapter is a summary of the stages and phases of generational secrets.) When a family grapples with its emotional difficulties, family members may think that if the people who held important secrets are dead, such secrets need not be revealed.

We disagree. Generational secrets are difficult to keep, even if they are not known on a conscious level. A family's past has a life of its own which no one escapes. Generation after generation, family members deal with the same personal terrors. This theme—that the sins of the father are visited upon the sons—has been a favorite in literature, explored by many of our greatest writers. We examine this concept through T. S. Eliot's play, *The Family Reunion,* and our clients' family histories. Family history is intricate and must be carefully explored. Research with surviving elders yields rich rewards for those with the patience to sift through stories, separating mythology from facts.

In *The Family Reunion,* Harry, the oldest son, comes home after a ten-year absence. He has returned to discover something from his boyhood that could revitalize his life. Harry's wife had died, swept overboard during an ocean voyage, and Harry is in anguish because he believes he may have pushed her into the sea. His pretentious mother, Amy, who has kept the family home exactly as it was when Harry left, hopes that Harry will live with her and that her relationship with him will resume where it left off.

Instead, Harry finds his mother's "arresting of the normal change of things" to be very unnatural. He thinks that "the instinct to return to the point of departure/ And start again as if nothing had happened" is folly. He realizes he cannot recapture his boyhood; nor, as he recovers memories of it, would he want to. Life at his mother's home is lived for form, not for adventure.

Harry is in a personal hell, an isolation, "irrevocable and irredeemable," recently supplanted by numbness, "the second hell of not being there," "the degradation of being parted from myself." At home, Harry realizes that the mystery of who he is lies in a generational secret.

He questions his aunt Agatha about his father, Chris, of whom he knows little. His aunt resists talking at first, but then confesses that Harry's parents' marriage was very unhappy. Both parents were lonely and isolated. But, the marriage contained an even more devastating secret.

When her sister was pregnant with Harry, Agatha discovered that Chris was plotting to murder his wife. Agatha changed Chris's mind by having an affair with him. But Chris's desire to kill Amy was real.

When Harry heard this story, he was relieved. He saw that his thoughts of pushing his own wife overboard were just fantasies. He says:

> "Perhaps my life has only been a dream
> Dreamt through me by the minds of others. Perhaps
> I only dreamt I pushed her."

Agatha is relieved to have been released from the burden she carried, but now she has transferred the burden to Harry. She tells him that she is frightened for him. Harry, however, is not. For the first time, he understands his feelings and his life.

> "Now I see
> I have been wounded in a war of phantoms
> Not by other human beings—they have no more power than I.
> The things I thought were real are shadows, and the real are what I thought were private shadows.
> O that awful privacy of the insane mind! Now I can live in public.
> Liberty is a different kind of pain from prison."

Agatha cautions against this youthful exuberance, but Harry is not ready to hear it. But Agatha is right: revealed secrets carry new responsibilities. The path to truth is not without peril and agony. But for Harry it is the path of life: the truth about his father's desire to kill his mother liberated Harry from the burden of the ancestral secret.

This play's message is familiar: the truth will set you free. When you don't know what went on in your family, you repeat past patterns, suffering the denied misery of previous generations. Harry understands his family, and feels compassion for them. He knows he must leave his unchanging home to pursue his own destiny.

In our work, we often see the damaging effects of a generational secret until separation occurs between our clients and their parents or ancestors. To achieve separation, the sin must be expiated. However, this can't happen until the sin is known. In Harry's case, the plot to murder his mother occurred while he was in utero, but still it affected his life. Our clients must investigate their past, question their parents, and discover what occurred in their childhood and in the childhood of their parents. Until this happens, they repeat the sins of the past.

Privacy of Parents versus Children's Right to Know

The following are very difficult questions to answer: What do children have the right to know? What is the private business of the parents? How do parents decide this? The answers are complex because they involve working through the shame parents feel about secrets, combined with decisions about the timing and appropriateness of telling. Children are not ready for some kinds of information until they have reached appropriate ages. In addition, some information is the province of the parent and need never belong to the child. The challenge for parents is to come to grips with the repetition, generation after generation, of the same family themes. Children have the right to know the truth of their generational history even if it is painful. Being a family member gives one rights.

Generational Stories

When Yvette, a vivacious, successful, forty-eight-year-old career woman, came to see us, she thought her main emotional problem was Ben, her fifty-one-year-old boyfriend, who had recently left her for a younger woman. Ben had done this four years before. In spite of this, Yvette thought Ben was a wonderful lover and her biggest fan "whenever he was around." She thrived on his compliments. But as she discussed this relationship with us, she neglected the obvious wounds Ben inflicted on her by discussing his dalliances in detail. "I know he sees me as special, but I never have had any leverage or rights with him," she said. Ben delighted in being seductive with everyone around him. To say he was charming was an understatement. He thought of himself as a person who wanted to make others happy. In fact, he was a seducer, who guarded his independence from Yvette and from his children by a previous marriage.

As we explored Yvette's unusual tolerance for her lover's wandering ways, she recalled that affairs were relatively common in her parents' lives. Yvette reviewed her memories and realized that her parents were also masters of charm. They were rather disinterested in child raising, and Yvette had gotten used to relationships where the focus was not on her. In addition, her parents' marriage had been a result of a torrid affair that broke up each of their first marriages. Yvette's father told her of his feelings of desperate excitement about her mother before she became an alcoholic. The generational pattern was continuing in Yvette's life. Her first husband, the father of her two children, was also an alcoholic. Yvette's desperate feelings for Ben mimicked those her father had for her mother.

Yvette's big secret emerged in our next session. When she was twenty-nine, and her daughter eight, her mother joined them on a trip to the family home in North Carolina. One evening as they flipped through the family album, Yvette found a snapshot of a young girl her mother couldn't identify. Later that night, Yvette's aunt explained that the girl was Yvette's half sister, torn from their mother by a divorce decree based on adultery. This sister had died of pneumonia when she was twenty.

Yvette never spoke about her half sister to her mother before she died. She realized that her mother's melancholy and alcoholism helped her avoid the enormous pain of abandoning a child. Yvette came to think that her mother had taught her to be emotionally invulnerable. She said, "I know I loved Ben and still want to be with him sometimes, but I don't think I have ever let myself be truly vulnerable to him." Yvette's breakthrough came when she became aware that she was vulnerable with Terry. This occurred while telling Terry a story about how she had raged at a friend who had not saved her a place to sit in a restaurant. She was embarrassed by her behavior, but, for the first time, Yvette willingly exposed her shame to Terry.

Where her mother and Ben used seduction, Yvette now learned to ask for what she wanted and not accept vague responses to her requests. She reassured herself that she did not need to settle for unhappiness "just to have somebody in my bed."

Yvette also found inspiration in acknowledging that her parents had had such a great love for each other that they left their marriages. Using this memory, she forgave herself for the shame she felt for accepting Ben's behavior and staying with him. She realized that she had been living with her mother's and her half sister's grief by accepting repeated abandonment.

Parents think they protect their children by not telling them about the past. Harry's mother thought so. So did Yvette's. But at some level, children seem to know about the skeletons in the closets. Generational secrets cast a long shadow, and it is usually life enhancing to know them.

Bill is another example of the power of generational secrets. He was thirty-nine when he came into psychotherapy after four years of abstention from alcohol. Although he had done some emotional healing in AA, he was still at the "In the Soup" stage and had a host of problems: Bill didn't trust women; he told himself that masturbation was sufficient to satisfy his sexual needs, but he didn't really believe it; he didn't like his job as a computer repair technician and had recently been laid off. He was cynical and depressed. He was in therapy only because his younger sister, Cindy, a successful patent lawyer, had forced him to go.

By accident, Bill's secret was revealed. In the exploration of why his family kept having children when he felt so unwanted, Bill recalled that there had been a stillborn son between him and his older brother. He asked his mother for more information about that time. His mother confessed that she had lived in dread throughout her pregnancy with Bill. After the previous death, she had not wanted to be pregnant again, but her religious beliefs prohibited her from using birth control. Bill worked with us to imagine the experience of being in utero with fear and rejection all around him. This was how he had felt his entire life.

After this exercise Bill felt enormous relief. His life of depression and the inhibitions on his assertiveness were explained. He and everyone in the family believed that he was simply a loser, a sharp contrast to his ambitious younger sister. Now Bill knew he was not. Bill still had a hard road ahead. He had enormous anger to work through and he had to grieve for thirty-nine years of self-blame. His mother had been caught in a moral dilemma of her own and he easily forgave her. His life now made sense to him, though, and he could move forward without apology or blame. For the first time, his life felt like his own. This does not mitigate the frustration that he had carried in his heart. He needed the energy of those feelings to move forward in his emotional healing.

The next story illustrates how untruths inevitably reemerge. Parents can say that they want a child but children know the truth. Molly, a thirty-five-year-old school-teacher, came to us because she was unhappy over the breakup of her eight-year marriage to her husband, Ted. She was comfortable about her decision to divorce and clearly was in stage 4, "The Telling Works." Yet, she was concerned about the effect of the divorce on her two young daughters. She also felt shame about a secret she had kept from Ted.

Early in their marriage Molly had wanted a child and Ted did not. When they had been apart for several weeks, Molly lied to Ted about her fertile dates, deliberately getting him to make love to her without protection.

Nine months later their oldest daughter, Sarah, was born. Molly knew that Ted's relationship with Sarah was not particularly loving. She felt very much to blame. Honesty was important to Molly and she couldn't understand what had possessed her to trick Ted.

Several months after we first met Molly, her mother died. On her deathbed, Molly's mother made a confession. She told Molly that while she was dating Molly's father, he had been drafted into the army during World War II. Afraid that he would be killed, he had not wanted to marry before shipping out. So her mother had gotten pregnant with Molly in order to force his hand.

Molly was stunned, but relieved. For the first time she could look at her tricking Ted as a subconscious repetition of her mother's behavior. She also understood why her father did not love her as much as he loved her younger brother and sister. With this revelation, Molly found compassion for herself. Using the Life Enhancement Grid, she decided to tell Ted what she had done and asked for his forgiveness. They couldn't put their marriage back together, but once Ted understood what motivated Molly, he felt more love for Sarah and became more careful about not acting out his resentments toward her.

When Generational Secrets Are Revealed

Simply knowing a generational secret is not absolute protection against repeating the sins of your ancestors. Only hard work loosens the bonds and clarifies your own motivations and behavior. Before you know what the secret is, however, you cannot even begin to do this work. Here is an example that Terry uncovered while at stage 6, "Secrets to Tell, Secrets to Keep."

TERRY: "I have always lived with anxiety about money even though there is plenty of it to make a good life for myself and my family. Sometimes this anxiety shows up around being taken advantage of by another or not getting a fair price, but mostly it's the fear of humiliation which, in my case, is being caught without enough. Even after I became relatively confident that I could earn a living and support our household, my financial fears persisted.

"One day I was listening to another therapist in a workshop. The therapist thought that my overwhelming fears might not be mine, but my father's or mother's. His premise was that children can bare their feelings when given support and focused attention, but when they are exposed to the unresolved feelings of their parents, they 'sponge up' these feelings. Since the feelings absorbed by the children are not their own, they become overhelming and must be defended against.

"The therapist pointed me in a very useful direction. Both my parents had grown up during the Depression. In the face of financial troubles brought on by this national calamity, my mother's family struggled to continue the appearance that everything was okay. The appearance of financial security was maintained by renting instead of buying a home and keeping their children in private school while being extremely careful with all other expenses, including food. My father had been brought up with money, but his career was created for him by his father. This fueled his insecurity which he expressed by acting overly self-important around his children. His fears were later compounded by his progressively debilitating alcoholism which eroded his job performance. I wondered if my father lacked the confidence that he could take care of his own without *his* father's support and money. His alcoholism had killed him long before I felt my own financial concerns.

"The therapist helped me set up a psychodrama during which I talked to another person who pretended to be my father. Almost immediately I was enraged, but I also gave him a clear message to keep his fears to himself. As I spoke on, I recalled the way Dad would sit with a tall glass of vodka and water, endlessly reading the financial and business news. I could also see in myself his paranoia about other people's motives. I remembered the strange way Dad would offer me cash as I was going out the door when I was home for a visit, long after I had stopped being financially dependent on him. I never knew how to respond. I realized it was his way of saying 'I love you,' but at the same time I resented it. I did not enjoy being dependent on my dad any more than he did on his.

"The therapist encouraged me to express that I did not wish to carry my father's fears any longer. I thanked my father for his generosity to me. I raged that I had lived with so much confusion that this fear had become a way of life for both of us. The fear helped kill him, but it was not going to destroy me or my marriage if I could help it."

When you know the themes that traumatize a family for generations, you can make life-enhancement choices. In the following story, the theme was "Always keep the family together, especially in the face of tragedy." When she first came to see us, Kendra, a twenty-four-year-old graduate student, was in stage 3, "Telling the Secret." A generational secret helped Kendra stand up for herself.

In Kendra's family, several generational secrets were shared openly. She and her sisters grew up knowing about the lives of her grandparents, and understanding the family themes. Kendra's grandfather, Gary, married a beautiful young woman named Elizabeth. When she became ill and died, he was heartbroken. He convinced Elizabeth's sister Beatrice, who had been his secretary, to become his wife. It was a marriage of convenience, never free from the memory of Elizabeth. They even named their daughter, Kendra's mother, Elizabeth.

When Kendra divorced her husband, George, her sister Hillary became involved in his life. Hillary's original motive was to see Kendra's children, but Hillary found herself swept into a relationship with George. Kendra was conflicted: she was jealous, but also wanted Hillary to be close to her children. In working through her emotional turmoil, she decided that it was life enhancing to make Hillary aware of re-creating the family secret. Both she and Kendra were impressed by the power of the family dynamic. In addition, Hillary learned that she didn't need to be anyone's poor substitute. She deserved a life and love of her own. She was not Beatrice, and Kendra was not Elizabeth.

If you do not face generational secrets, you take on the family's wounds, carry the family's grieving in the form of depression, and repeat the family's crimes or spend your lifetime trying to atone for them. We encourage our clients to research their family history with living relatives to find out what they don't want to talk about. Sometimes longtime family friends or housekeepers have useful perspectives and memories. By framing your inquiry as an exploration of family history, older relatives will eventually share important stories. Questions like "What was my mother like as a girl?" and "Did that automobile accident happen before World War II?" can stimulate memories and keep you focused.

Family Myths

Myths envelop every family so as to create a sense of belonging. Positive ones are "Our family is blessed," and "We never get sick in our family." Negative ones include "We drink too much," and "We are afraid of success." Such negative familial identification affects a child. Most often these myths are not conscious; the family is not aware of its own beliefs. Part of healing is making these beliefs conscious, then a person can decide whether or not to continue acting as if they were true. When you don't know what motivates you, you are like a puppet whose strings are being pulled by unknown people and ideas.

Thirty-two-year-old Allan came to see us because his life was "a mess." Allan was "In the Soup." He was broke, out of work, and drinking heavily. The only son in a family of six girls, he, like his father, always had a hard time in school. Allan had been fired from several jobs, mainly because he never tried anything new. Whenever a boss wanted to expand his job description, Allan would get angry, refuse, and quit. He also had made several disastrous investments.

In our initial discussions, Allan talked a lot about his father, Stanley, who struggled to live up to *his* alcoholic father's demands and experienced one failure after another. When Allan was born, Stanley was a defeated man. Identifying with his father, Allan had bought into the family myth: "The men in this family are failures." By drinking he was also playing out the myth that "Alcoholism runs in this family."

As Allan grieved for the sadness of his father's life, and allowed himself to feel his anger toward his dad, he broke free from the family myths. As he did, Allan designed his own life-enhancing image. His myth was that he was born in the "Land of Failure," but through great struggle he had made it over the mountain into the green valley on the other side, which he called the "Land of Success and Satisfaction." Since being out-of-doors had always brought him great pleasure, Allan decided to go to school to become a ranger. Gradually, he straightened out his finances. When we last saw him, he was a happy man, fulfilled, and at peace with himself, no longer buying into any myth except those he created himself.

The Sense of Family Doom

Death was something Alice lived with every day as an emergency room nurse in a large urban hospital. Forty-eight years old, divorced, and with three grown children, Alice appeared tough but had a great sense of humor and a warm personality. The secrets that plagued her—loss and coping with loss—dovetailed nicely with her work in the emergency room. She was in stage 3, "Telling the Secret," when she came to our group sessions.

Alice had few clues as to what was bothering her when she entered psychotherapy. She sensed her life was going nowhere. She had been in a long-term relationship with a married man, Henry, who wasn't about to divorce. Henry said he did not want to divide his fortune, and his wife would not allow him to divorce because of religious beliefs. Alice did not leave Henry, even though she was confident that that was the next step. Alice was full of rationalizations: she and Henry had "so much fun" when he was available; he was "attentive and generous"; and there were "so few good men out there." Her unhappy first marriage confirmed Alice's gloomy thesis.

As we talked week after week, Alice revealed her family secret—death. A brother had died in childhood. Recently, another sibling had passed away of breast cancer, leaving small children. The widower was taking his children with him into a new marriage in the upcoming weeks, and Alice feared that she would not see her sister's children as much in the future. This, coupled with the support of group members, was the final straw that pushed Alice into stage 4, "The Telling Works."

Over the generations, Alice's family had forgotten how to grieve. They only knew how to move forward stoically, burying the dead and "fighting like hell for the living." This irreverence for death went back to the family emigration from Ireland, when the young left the old to die, and the very young died on the boats to America. The Roman Catholic Church provided solace to earlier generations, but not that of Alice's mother. She acted the role of devout Catholic when required, but then bitterly complained about her life to her children. Alice was repelled by this hypocrisy and drifted into a secular life, raising her own family outside the church.

After a year of therapy, Alice decided to break off with Henry. Afterwards, she and a friend took a vacation to Ireland to search for remnants of her family. Alice came back with the vitality of a lottery winner. While she found no direct connection to her ancestors other than some gravestones, she made friends in the pubs where her relatives once socialized and walked the streets they had once trod. While still relatively impoverished, these people were connected to their lives in a way that she was not. Alice found her spirituality in her grief and in the land of her ancestors.

Unlike Alice, the keeper of the following secret wanted to preserve the family from some sort of doom. Tom, a writer, learned a family secret at his uncle

Leonard's funeral. As Tom talked with Leonard's children, he discovered that they believed their grandfather had been dead for years. Incredulous, Tom told them that their grandfather had been living in an adjacent town until his death two years before. Tom knew Uncle Leonard had visited his father regularly and had supported him financially. Leonard's children were furious with their father for keeping this secret and depriving them of a grandfather. No one knew the reason for Leonard's deception; he took it to his grave. But we can imagine several scenarios. Perhaps the grandfather was senile. Or maybe he was an alcoholic, or a child abuser. Or maybe Leonard was angry at him for not being a good father, and punished him by depriving him of his grandchildren. Whatever it was, Leonard lived his life in a stage-2 silence that felt like betrayal to his children.

If Leonard's father was a child abuser or a violent alcoholic, then Leonard needed to protect his children, at least during their childhood. By the time they were teenagers, however, the family secrets could and ought to have been shared. Children have a right to their heritage. They want and need it, for it is part of their sense of belonging in the world. Knowing the family legacy gives children information that they can act on, just like the protagonist in Eliot's play. Without it, a useful caution light about such things as alcoholism or mental illness is missing. The tragedy of Leonard's story is that his children may never forgive him in the same way that Leonard did not forgive his own father.

Birth Secrets

Birth secrets are another example of secrets that children are not aware of but usually find life enhancing to know at a young age. Experts on adoption propose that adopted children should never remember a time when they did not know they were adopted. Later on, other relevant information, such as where the birth was, can be passed on when the child is ready and interested. In addition, an adopted child is encouraged to develop a healthy sense of privacy about the information. Thus, birth history does not become a source of shame to parents or children, even though it might be to the absent and unknown birth mother and father.

Birth secrets such as adoption and illegitimacy are powerful because they touch on a person's right to exist and to be part of a healthy relationship. A person needs a sense of what psychologists call affiliative trust—a deep trust in the capacity of a relationship to be fulfilling, consistent, and safe. Such a trust is usually (some say always) developed in the first years of life. Parents rupture such trust when they keep secrets of birth, or when they are so paralyzed by their own secrets that they cannot be fully emotionally available for the child. Parental discomfort, which is always communicated to children, either through action or omission, undermines healthy family relationships.

To see the impact of when birth secrets are not shared, let's look at Gino and Andrea's story. Gino, twenty-six, was unaware that he was not his father's child but the love child from an affair his mother secretly maintained for years. Revealing this secret would have probably blown the family apart. The mother eventually told Gino's older sister, Andrea. She had the name and number of Gino's father "in case of emergency."

Gino's life unconsciously mirrored its "love-child" origins. The mother doted on Gino, while she was highly critical of Andrea and her brother, Paul. Gino was impulsive and capable of doing harmful things to himself. He went from job to job, and had several bad motorcycle accidents. It was Andrea's task to rein him in, a responsibility she dreaded.

Not surprisingly, Gino's relationship with his alcoholic father was tense and cautious, even though neither knew the facts of Gino's birth. Gino assumed early in his life that his father didn't love him because he was inherently unlovable. He thought he was a bad kid, and he spent his life acting on his belief.

Andrea came to us shortly after Gino had had another motorcycle accident. Should she tell her brother about his past? As we talked, Andrea realized that if Gino knew the truth, he would finally have a context for something he had felt all his life. But Andrea had promised her mother to keep the secret, so there might be hell to pay if she broke her word. She also knew that there was no guarantee that the rage Gino might release wouldn't cut off everyone in the family, including her. After all, she had known for years and hadn't told. Would Gino take this information and drive his motorcycle even faster? Andrea was paralyzed with fear and rage.

Who Gets to Tell?

What do you do if you know a secret that a child doesn't know, and the child's parent isn't telling? Whose business is it to tell? Andrea struggled with this dilemma.

We took Andrea through the Life Enhancement Grid, asking her to check her body as she questioned herself about the effects of telling the secret. The secret felt like a terrible burden to her. Her life would be better if she shared it. Andrea also felt the instability of the family and her brother. Given her feelings, Andrea decided to wait. She was too afraid to "play God with [her] brother's life."

While we generally believe that generational secrets need to be told, we respected Andrea's courage and her careful exploration of this situation. So much was at stake. Andrea had no confidence in the emotional maturity of her family. The last thing she wished to do was make things worse. She decided, however, to challenge her mother to tell the secret that really was the mother's secret in the first place.

Secrets That Bind: Genetic Secrets

Some of what we inherit from our families is emotional, but some is biochemical. The tendency to be depressed, for example, can be passed down genetically, as can mania, schizophrenia, alcoholism, obesity, cancer, high-blood pressure, and so forth. Such family secrets are life enhancing to know, for a person then can act preventatively.

James's story illustrates this point well. James is a thirty-five-year-old, unmarried carpenter, addicted to marijuana and suffering depression. Discovering that his maternal grandmother had been administered shock treatments gave James the courage to find a doctor who diagnosed him with depression and placed him on medication. This lifted his spirits and helped him to stop smoking pot.

James's mother had not deliberately withheld this information from him; she had simply forgotten an unpleasant fact. James realized that depression was something that ran in his family. His mother and sister were often tearful and spent a lot of time locked in their rooms. Until he knew his depression was inherited, James thought his lack of energy was his own fault. He blamed himself for smoking marijuana instead of seeing it as his attempt to medicate himself for a biochemical imbalance. With knowledge came understanding and the motivation to find a solution. Telling secrets changed James's life for the better.

The Tangled Web a Family Can Weave: Doing Your Own Exploration

Anya is a friend of ours. Warm, good-hearted, and wacky, she has struggled mightily to make better sense of her relationships and actions. Recently, she told Karen this story about the role of secrets in her life, and how she had struggled to heal a deep, and for her, terrible generational wound.

In 1984, while traveling with a friend, Anya visited a Native American holy man named Samuel. The holy man, whose wife had left him some eight years before for a younger man, was suffering from lung cancer that would eventually result in his death. During this visit, Anya and Samuel, who were the same age, connected strongly. Anya, in fact, had left her own husband and adolescent children to pursue her own personal recovery from the loneliness and spiritual emptiness that existed in her marriage. She had become aware of her responsibility in damaging the marriage because she ignored problems and was often self-righteous and hostile. Anya helped Samuel accept why his wife may have had to leave to heal her own wounds.

Anya also responded to Samuel's desire to bring back the ancient traditions of his tribe. He had begun a

traditional council to provide a place for dialogue between the different age groups in the community, and he
had built a "round" house to reestablish spiritual ways.
Although Samuel often dressed in a way that was fitting
to his position as holy man—an immaculately beaded
white suit decorated with feathers and turquoise—he and
his family lived in poverty. His house had neither running
water nor an indoor toilet. Samuel and three of his children lived in three rooms. Recognizing that Samuel was
dying and that he had limited financial resources, Anya
decided to assist him.

One day Samuel invited Anya to help put on a Youth
and Elders conference. She agreed to supply food for the
gathering. A disaster followed. Anya's daughter, Alexis,
accompanied her, but she left after one day. Alexis acqui-
esced to the hostile attitude of the young male Native
Americans who said they didn't want any whites present
during the council.

ANYA: "Something in me needed to stay. The connection with the women and children was important; there
was a strong core developing there. But the men treated
me like a dog. They made me fry bread. I stood for hours
over the hot grease, my arms being burned by the spat-
tering fat. I got to experience the other side of victimiza-
tion and exploitation. I imagined that this was some kind
of a spiritual test. The Native Americans made fun of my
ways, and frightened me with the energy of their traditional dances."

When a violent thunderstorm erupted, Anya retreated to her tent and cowered in fear. Later, when she
emerged, only two men on security were awake.

ANYA: "I felt like a kid, getting to stay up with the grown-ups. They teased me for being afraid and laughed at me, but it was a gentle laughing. I felt safe with them. It was as if something got released in me that night, something was healed."

Shortly after Anya arrived home from the conference, she learned that her brother had just discovered a book written by Robert Linsey called *The Reason for the Tears,* an historical account of the forced march of the Indians out of the Southeast to Oklahoma. Samuel's tribe was part of the march. She was stunned by the link. Even more disturbing was that her family was mentioned several times in the book. By the time Anya was born, her relatives were "a grand old family" who saw themselves as better than other people. *The Reason for the Tears,* however, said that the family had come to this country with James Oglethorpe, who had brought with him people from debtors' prisons. Early family members had mined limestone for a living, pulling it by hand to boats.

As Anya's research continued, more secrets emerged. The grand old family had a history of debts and, later, of exploitation. They had raped the earth, first by mining limestone, then by growing cotton, which depletes the soil, and later drilling for oil. Anya's family had made its fortune by swindling Native Americans, and later African Americans, who by the time Anya began her healing journey, were so poor that only the emotionally impaired remained in the community. "It is still a slave system," Anya said.

Suddenly Anya's meeting Samuel, even being treated like a dog, made sense. It was part of an expiation, a moment for her to experience firsthand what her family, along with other whites, had put Native Americans through. Filled with a sense of spiritual renewal, Anya threw herself into the study of her family history. She talked to anyone who could fill out the story for her, from family to friends to longtime servants. More secrets tumbled out. Some of the grand dames of the family were lesbians, a fact never mentioned. She also remembered her father confessing that he had belonged to the Ku Klux Klan. There were other dark secrets: half-remembered images of sexual abuse, and an angry black nanny who retaliated against Anya and her brother for the pain whites had brought.

ANYA: "The rest of the family still thinks that we are a grand old family. Neither of my brothers admit that most of us were alcoholics. They'd never agree that we exploited people to make money. I am sure that there are plenty more secrets that have never come out, but I don't even know what they are.

"The secrets made me crazy. I didn't know what was real and what was fantasy. The money made me crazy, too, because it kept me from reality. Recently I remembered being raped as a child. That memory has given me great relief because I understand now what that rape did to my soul. My life now makes sense. I understand now why I couldn't express myself without making something up that I thought would protect me by pleasing other people."

Anya still believed she needed to do more healing. For this to happen, she needed to know more truths. What was her family's exact role in destroying the ways of Native Americans? How many crimes of the past rested on her head? The truth, Anya believed, would make her free. But it isn't only truth. She also imagined she needed to make restitution. "I have felt so much shame my whole life, I wonder if it comes from the crimes of the past," she said. The contrast between what Anya had always been told about her family—that they were upstanding, and somehow better than others—with what she had discovered about their behavior ripped apart the fabric of her emotional life. "The discrepancies have continued down to this generation and frightened me. I would not tell my relatives about my discoveries and my suspicions because I am afraid they would think me crazy and lock me up," Anya remarked.

Anya believed these secrets and could no longer live the lie and stay sane. In her family investigation, Anya developed a new awareness of her mother, who was supposed to have been the "crazy one" in the family. With her discoveries, Anya concluded that her mother became that way because she didn't leave her husband and pursue her own life. Her father was the crazy and abusive one. Her mother's tragedy was that she didn't listen to her own truth, but kept the family secrets and stayed so the family would look good. Anya appreciated her mother's courage. She decided, in the end, that it would be life enhancing to keep her truth to herself and tell it only to her children when they were old enough to hear it. Anya hoped to expiate the sins of her fathers and create a new myth for her life. She was working now on becoming The-One-Who-Put-It-Right.

Anya realized that the crimes of the past are not hers, and she worked hard to distance herself from the attitudes and destructive ways of life of many of her family members. The discovery that her own passions are kindled by knowing the truth surprised her. Her anger was no longer "against" her family and racism, but became more and more focused "for" human rights and community building. And while she cannot remedy the past or improve others' futures, she could live in a different way and that, for her, was most gratifying.

Generational Secrets

	DISCOVERY	CATHARSIS	INDIVIDUATION
1. *In the Soup*	I struggle with meaning in life.	Either I have emotional outbursts or I withdraw in silence.	I will not be bound by my family's legacy.
2. *Shame Keeps You Silent*	I have no clue what my family secrets are or who is keeping them. Loyalty keeps me silent.	I discover the significance of generational secrets.	I am alone, but I can find out my family legacy.
3. *Telling the Secret*	I research my past by interviewing surviving family members and exploring attics and old family albums.	I am involved in intense emotional work wherein the focus is, "Who am I like?"	I am in a fellowship with others who are on the same path. We share our stories.
4. *The Telling Works*	I begin to see the pattern repeated—suffering through the generations.	Through intense emotional work, I strive for independence from the legacy of shame.	I now know the truth, but I don't blame others.
5. *Stuck in the Telling*	I avoid family members and overvalue the healing process. I am feeling too vulnerable to deal with family.	I work through my fear of nontherapeutic aspects of my life. I am often consumed by anger.	I take responsibility for my life. I take risks with family members.
6. *Secrets to Tell, Secrets to Keep*	I experiment with new behavior. I set boundaries with unhealthy family members.	I enjoy risk taking. I detach from my family and its drama, using the Life Enhancement Grid.	I state my truth, and develop courage to walk my own path.
7. *Freedom*	I enjoy my family history.	I have gratitude for life's lessons, however painful.	I feel a deep connection to those I love.

7

Family Secrets

*"When I was seven years old, I kept no secrets
from [my mother] and spoke to her with complete
freedom. . . . After that my attitude changed.
Prudence counseled us to hold our tongues."*

—SIMONE DE BEAUVOIR

Every family is a cauldron of secrets. Problems
occur when a child cannot share a concern
about a secret with a parent as it happens.
Eventually that concern turns into a long-term problem
and a source of shame. The mismanagement of secrets in
families degenerates into long-term destructive behaviors
which are passed on to the next generation.

The chart of the stages and phases of family secrets
at the end of the chapter highlights this tragedy. An alternative is to create a "new family," with a focus on personal change. Whether with friends or as a client of a
therapist, the "new family" becomes a sacred circle that
provides relief from old family patterns. Unfortunately,
these new patterns of behavior can be thwarted by members of one's family of origin even when you only talk to
them on the phone or see them occasionally.

In healthy families, children learn a balanced sense

of what is life enhancing to disclose or keep private. As we saw in the last chapter, some secrets can last for lifetimes. In troubled homes, children naturally take on family shame and shoulder responsibility for keeping family secrets from outsiders. Within such families, no one talks about real problems, and one or both parents display some of the following symptoms:

- Is physically or emotionally abusive
- Drinks excessively or is frequently drunk
- Is drugged or spaced-out on pills
- Has crying fits
- Spends most of the day in bed
- Is unable to keep the house in order
- Has trouble staying employed
- Has a desire to fight
- Is unable to display love

Our clients who grew up in families with a lot of physical and verbal abuse, for instance, must expose the secret that their parents were out of control. Telling a secret to a therapist, as we have already shown, yields far more positive results than the high-stakes endeavor of confronting a parent about actions taken long ago.

Let's look at some examples of family secrets. The first one involves family secrets that were well known to the family members but were never discussed. If they had been, their meaning could have been shared and feelings could have been expressed and attended to.

Leslie was a fifty-year-old administrator in a large corporation when we met her. She had enjoyed an independent life and had had a number of sexual relationships that had ended without marriage. She seemed close to her mother with whom she shared a triple-decker house. But, there was a family secret that Leslie had spent her life denying, which was that there was only bitterness in her family. When her mother died, Leslie realized she could not hide from this secret anymore. Her mother had used her matriarchal power to suppress any discussion of family acrimony. At her mother's funeral, Leslie's siblings let their anger out, and then quickly went their separate ways. Leslie was left with the triple-decker house and little else.

LESLIE: "I had spent my life believing that family is important and cultivating the myth that my family was close. I lived in an apartment downstairs from my mother and enjoyed being available to help her at any given moment. Being single and my mother's assistant and companion, I never moved on. When she died, the bubble burst. I had nothing in common with my six siblings, other than memories. Now I see that these memories were filled with little resentments and personal offenses that my mother smoothed over.

"No one ever asks me over, and I only have contact with a niece and a nephew at holidays. I am shocked at how distant my family is. I feel sad and hurt. I did all the cooking for holiday dinners while my mother was alive, keeping up the illusion that we were a happy family. Now I know who my friends are, and I live my life accordingly."

Leslie was taken by surprise when her mother died because she didn't know anything different and she loved the image she had of her family. Grieving the loss of her siblings came readily to her as she began her emotional healing. Her mother had been firm and cold, but fortunately she also had been emotionally present, attentive, and consistent, leaving Leslie with a fairly good sense of her own identity. The role of the dutiful daughter had served her well in some ways, especially professionally. She was a loyal and appreciated employee of a respected company and had sufficient money to enjoy a good lifestyle. Using the Life Enhancement Grid, Leslie decided that it was too late—and would require too much energy—to resolve the issues that ripped her family apart. She wanted to get on with her life. Her time was too precious to be wasted on family members she hardly knew.

The Element of Trust in a Family

Leslie trusted the family myth and found herself in crisis when her mother died. For her it was a good crisis. Not every person is so lucky as to sustain a secret until he or she has the maturity to deal with it. A phrase we use in our workshops and lectures is, "This is the only Mommy and Daddy you are ever going to have." A child's basic assumption is that her or his parents knew what they were doing. When inconsistencies arise in the parents' behavior and language, a child's tendency is to either ask why (if she or he feels safe enough) or to "make it work" in her or his own mind. The goal is to minimize the terrifying thought that Mommy and Daddy might not be healthy individuals with your best interest in mind.

Adrienne Rich in her book *On Lies, Secrets and Silence* states a valuable creed for any family: "I have faith that you are telling things it is important I should know; that you do not conceal facts from me in an effort to spare me, or yourself, pain." This creed holds for children, as well as parents, because often early in life children have learned the taboo against talking of painful things.

In our next story, Suzanne did not trust her mother enough to get the help she needed. The secrets we keep often reflect our level of trust. Having too much trust is just as problematic as having too little.

Not Having Enough Trust

Some secrets that cause us to suffer involve events we remember, but many secrets involve events that we have forgotten. Due to the psyche's instinct to protect itself, the mechanism of repression banishes painful memories from conscious thought. Repressing an event, however, does not mean that we are free from it. On the contrary, what is unconscious is more dangerous than what we know because it directs our life without our awareness.

Suzanne, thirty, worked in retail women's apparel and looked the part. You would never know that she repressed secrets unless you were one of the many men trying unsuccessfully to become involved with her. Suzanne didn't have close female friends either. She focused her energy on work and her psychotherapy, and felt stuck in her habit of being a "happy girl," leading a life devoid of satisfaction. For months in therapy Suzanne had flashes of memory, little snippets of an event from her childhood, something troubling and difficult, that always eluded definition. Perhaps, she thought, it was a memory of sexual abuse. It had that quality of strobelike glimpses accompanied with anxiety.

We encouraged her to go slowly, and reassured her that she wasn't making it up. Our working assumption was that if Suzanne believed something was there, it was.

We do not, however, push for memories, which we believe can be made up to explain strong emotions. False memories are dangerous because they create extremely debilitating feelings. Ours is an open and balanced view of memory retrieval work. Talking to others about memories, or accusing perpetrators, are separate choices that should come after emotional work has had time to settle. Then, life-enhancement decisions can be made with equanimity.

One day Suzanne was having a deep-tissue massage and turned her attention to the musculature of her legs and pelvis. She found an area of tightening, a tensing of the muscles in her hip that she could not relax. Slowly she allowed herself to enter the tension until feelings flooded her. She was filled with fear. Reassured by the massage therapist, Suzanne let the fear grow in her until her whole body shook. Tears flooded her eyes. Old images flashed in her mind, but more slowly now. Suzanne began to recognize the shapes. There was her father. He looked big. She could see the brown bars of her crib. She recognized the blue wallpaper of her nursery.

"Let yourself be there," her massage therapist said. Suzanne found herself looking up at her father, who was looming over her head. She was a toddler in her crib. What was happening? She felt her baby body. Her hip was burning, and her whole body tensed in terror and disbelief. What had happened? Where was Mom? As Suzanne worked with the images and feelings that came to her, she recovered a vivid memory.

Dad had been changing her. He didn't like to do it, she could tell by the tension in his body and the look on his face. But her mother wasn't there. Suzanne was a typical frisky two-year-old who seldom held still for diaper changes. Her father, exasperated with her squirming, slapped her hard. Suzanne began to cry immediately, but something menacing in her father's expression caused her to stop quickly. At that moment, they both heard her mother approaching. Suzanne and her dad were frozen in a tableau of complicity. Suzanne stifled her tears. Her father was startled. They both pretended nothing bad had happened.

This became the critical secret of Suzanne's childhood. The scene was repeated again and again as she grew up. Abused by her angry father, she kept it a secret from her mother, burying the hurt deep within her body. She knew her father was frustrated with his life and so made excuses for him. Suzanne was alone, unable to turn for solace to her mother, who had to be protected from this awful knowledge, and who seemed to be insensitive to Suzanne's feelings anyway.

So much was explained by this story: Suzanne now had an explanation for why her body seemed to freeze whenever a man came near. She also understood her lack of deep relationships with women: female friendships always felt like an act on her part. Now she began to have some choice about how she would relate to people, instead of unconsciously repeating this childhood scene. The discovery of her secret complicity with her father enabled her to make many more conscious choices.

When a child like Suzanne keeps a family secret, she learns a lot of things, none of which serve her well in her adult life. These include:

1. *Improper loyalty:* Suzanne had found herself keeping unnecessary secrets in her adult life and tolerated abuse without exposing the abuser. This perpetuated harmful situations as an adult, just as her loyalty to her father resulted in her tolerating his abuse and made her unable to reach out to her mother for help. As an adult, she could act in her best interest; as a child, she could not.

2. *Improper trusting:* Suzanne learned to bury her feelings and deny her distrust of the perpetrator. Rather than admit how much her father hurt her and reach out to her mother, she failed to develop trust in her own protective abilities. She developed pain-avoidant coping mechanisms (denial, blaming herself, addiction to excitement, etc.) rather than face her pain and trust that an open family relationship would yield satisfaction. Later in life she would say, "It doesn't bother me," rather than stand up for herself.

3. *Improper self-sacrifice:* Suzanne denied her own needs in order to put her mother and father first. This tendency continued into her adulthood as she became stuck in caretaking patterns, always neglecting herself. Suzanne paid little attention to the potential rewards of a good friendship that are created by opening one's inner life to another.

4. *Inaccurate life-enhancement decisions:* Suzanne didn't tell her secret because she wanted to protect both her parents from the pain of dealing with her father's anger. But she also learned to fear the humiliation that she thought would come her way if she were to tell. Her mother often criticized Suzanne when she reached out in need. Suzanne usually kept quiet rather than be ridiculed. In the middle of her therapy, Suzanne confided in her mother. To her surprise, Suzanne found that her mother had felt excluded from Suzanne's life. Her mother had been aware all along of Suzanne's problems with her father and had used criticism to stifle any attempt by Suzanne to discuss the problem. Ironically, Suzanne's mother cut herself off from what she desired most: warm contact with her daughter. A family therapist could have easily helped this family by simply identifying the "rhinoceros in the living room"—the father's frustration with his life.

5. *Inaccurate assessment of reality:* Suzanne learned to compulsively deny reality. Eventually, she couldn't recognize what she really felt about anything. Thinking "it wasn't so bad" and "it didn't hurt me" was so ingrained in her that knowing what her feelings were became impossible, especially with men she found attractive.

6. *Failure to develop healthy boundaries:* Suzanne's inability to say no to her father, led to an inability to say no to everyone. Her personal boundaries were so poorly established that she often became the whipping girl of her female acquaintances and the one taken for granted, and sometimes even the abused woman to her sexual partners.

7. *Inappropriate projection of parental truths:* Another common result of repressed family secrets is projection onto friends and lovers of a person's own secrets. In Suzanne's case, the abuse she suffered at her father's hands made her so afraid that she projected his rage onto every man she met. If there was any anger in a man at all, she would see it, missing the parts of him that were loving and kind. If an alliance between a mother and daughter is not strong, and it wasn't in this case, that daughter may grow up believing that all her friends compete with her and are not sources of support. This then also affected her friendships with women.

In projection, the secret is often our own feelings. An example of this is when a child, furious with his or her parents, cannot admit it. Instead, the child projects the anger onto dolls, invisible friends, and stuffed animals. Another example is when a woman cannot admit her own sexual desires, so she imagines that every man she meets desires her.

Shame in Families

Shame was at the core of the psychological mechanisms that made Suzanne choose to keep her secrets from herself and her mother. Although she did not know it at the beginning of her emotional healing, she inhibited most of her genuine self-expression in favor of her "happy girl" mask. As we stated earlier, shame is the underbelly of the individual's attempt to live up to an unreal image of how things should be. In Suzanne's case, the image is, "Dad and I love each other and get along very well." It reflects a betrayal of the true self, of which Suzanne was unconsciously ashamed. The true self was enraged and terrified by her father's ever present frustration with his life.

Yet, we must not make the mistake of blaming the victim who carries shame. In this case, healing occurred when Suzanne accepted her father's actions for what they were—abuse of the most vulnerable person in the family. Naming a crime does not mean confronting the perpetrator—an act that may be important to some, but is not essential to healing—rather, it means telling oneself the truth, including the sadness, fear, and rage that one has buried. Having a witness present often helps this process. But remember, healing takes time because the images a person has held for a lifetime must be repeatedly challenged.

Shame becomes incorporated into the child's psyche in such a way that there is no easy exit. The child senses that his or her real self has no right to exist or, at best, has little value to his or her parents. Because of this, secrets involving shame, whether repressed or kept consciously, are extremely dangerous. When we think something in the privacy of our own mind, the very act of thinking it makes us believe it is true. The only way to verify the truth or falsity of a thought is to tell someone else and expose it to the light of day. If we don't, the secret (or thought) becomes more powerful, threatening to escape. We have to hold it in. Pretty soon, we are expending enormous energy and living with constant fear. We depend on total denial to continue this effort. Eventually, we may break down completely.

In dysfunctional families like Suzanne's, there was no validation for her experience of abuse because she never asked for it. In other families, children are lied to and even blamed for their own discomfort (e.g., "You shouldn't feel that way" or "If you hadn't provoked me, I wouldn't have hit you").

We feel relieved when we share our pain. Something we think about and stew over may seem monumental until it is told; then, it reduces itself to the small problem that it really is. Discussing the story may reveal further memories or an angle not seen before that allows resolution.

Healthy families have safe and constructive ways of giving focused attention to everyone's emotional life. In "shame-based families," as John Bradshaw calls them, shame is used to silence truth-tellers. Being shamed is the experience of being hated, nothing less. Usually the child's ego attempts to minimize the effect of shame with such meager defenses as rationalizing that "Mommy and Daddy really do love me" or attacking a beloved toy with the same shaming message. But this does little to help the child escape the trauma that carries this message: *We, your family, who are closest to you and know you best, are not interested in the real you. Why should anyone else be? You better learn to be secretive.*

This message, unfortunately, often works until a person becomes emotionally attached to a lover or to his or her own children. It works because control of the self and others takes priority over emotional closeness and feeling. In intimate relationships, however, the intensity of the involvement breaks down the shamed individual's carefully constructed images. Then, either one of two things happen: (1) the shamed adult has childlike temper tantrums, or (2) the person shames loved ones in the same way that she or he was shamed. This next story illustrates how buried shame pops out unexpectedly.

Sandra, an energetic and attractive thirty-five-year-old chemistry professor, was the oldest of eight children. Sandra's father, Albert, had a long history of depression, the causes of which were never explored. His children's support and concern seemed to mean little to him. Occasionally suicidal, he was the focus of endless family discussions and attention. Sandra's mother had been dedicated to raising her large family and was "exhausted beyond her years." This family was masterful at keeping up appearances and denying the significance of the numerous setbacks that the children repeatedly were going through (e.g., trouble in school, depression, and unfulfilled intimate relationships).

When Sandra started therapy, she had a sense that her family history had affected her. Although doing well in her career, she had enormous trouble sustaining relationships beyond what she called "the six-month hump." She had no idea what she was doing wrong. Sandra quickly discovered that her goal was to be a perfect partner for her lovers. As she molded her desires to conform to what they liked, she suppressed her hurts and angers.

Her anxious desire to be perfect was probably obvious to her lovers, but she couldn't understand why they rejected her. She was "so good to them."

In therapy she initially focused on her current crisis involving boyfriend trouble or on her family's difficulties. Challenged to describe the painful events of her past, the critical secret emerged. When Sandra was nine and her brother was six, they had been asked to watch their two-year-old sister Molly. Tragically, Molly followed a flock of ducks into a pond in their backyard and drowned.

The family's spirit never recovered. Sandra's parents went on separate vacations within three weeks of the drowning, each taking different children. Healing the grief never occurred because the family felt so much shame and guilt. No one talked openly about the drowning.

Several weeks after this revelation, Sandra told us that recently her mother confessed that Sandra's father had been "passed out from drinking" when Molly drowned. By this point in therapy, Sandra understood that she and her brother were too young to be responsible for a two-year-old child. She also grasped that her mother and father shamed their children to minimize their own sense of guilt for not attending to their duties.

With this knowledge, Sandra connected her repressed grief to her obsessive perfectionism and to her inability to be open with her lovers. She was, however, unable to talk about her sister's death with the family. No one wanted to think or hear about it, let alone encourage Sandra's parents to address their own buried grief and guilt. The reaction she received was that she was being a "bossy big sister" when she talked about her own emotional work.

Secret Worlds versus the Real World

The horror of a two-year-old's death is so enormous that compassion for Sandra's family is warranted, but their style of coping cannot work. The greater the discrepancy between the real world and a secret world a child invents to deal with emotional pain, the greater the shame. The child goes back into the real world only to interact carefully with it, never to feel safe in it. Without a feeling of safety and enthusiasm for living, the only meaning within a family comes from what we call adrenalized crisis management. Such families focus on solving the next problem and thrive on the voyeurism that is fueled by revealing others' secrets.

Let's look at an example of this. At the time we met Janice, she was forty-eight and had a job she enjoyed as a maternity assistant. Her husband, Reed, was sober, kind, and employed. She had struggled through her own childhood with two alcoholic parents, and then married and eventually divorced the alcoholic father of her five children. Janice prided herself in rising above the chaos.

Janice also had some obvious problems. Her compulsive need to keep a clean house irritated everyone: her, Reed, and her teenage children. Her positive self-image that "[she's] at her best in crisis" was developed on the shaky ground of too many crises and too much shame throughout her life. She had a reasonably satisfying life, but she was unconsciously creating crises where there was no need for them. In the secret world inside her mind, she was a heroine who rescued those in need. But Janice was now facing the midlife event that her children didn't need her anymore. Her family was tired of her martyring herself on a cross that no one wanted her to carry.

In psychotherapy, Janice quickly uncovered her secrets. She carried a secret belief that her family was some sort of "bad seed." While wishing to be "a good Catholic," Janice secretly imagined her family was "possessed by the devil" and that her job was to wrestle with this devil.

One of her earliest memories was the sign outside her house that announced the foreclosure auction of her home. As Janice told us: "I don't know what happened to all my friends after that. I doubt their families were doing a great deal better, but I was treated as if foreclosure was contagious." Janice was so ashamed that she didn't rage at the injustice being done to her and her siblings. Drinking was apparently a higher priority for her folks than shelter.

Janice had another secret. She had never admitted it, but she had purposely become pregnant. Janice hoped that marriage and a family would protect her and provide the decent life denied her by her parents. But these choices only brought new struggles, which, in turn, distracted her from facing up to her rage. She was angry all the time, but something or somebody was always the cause of her anger. Slowly she accepted her anger and that events were excuses to "vent [her] spleen."

As Janice examined her anger, she became less stressed by daily life. She focused instead on negotiating constructively with friends and family. Shame became a feeling she could now name, allowing her to let go of the image of herself as a heroine in a life-and-death struggle. Now she could relax and think about cultivating joy in herself and those around her.

Her cleaning compulsions had been designed to make everything all right in the eyes of God, rather than to get along with others in the world. Janice knew that she would always prefer everything to be clean, but now she could pat herself on the back for letting things go for a day or two.

Janice decided to not tell anyone about the fantasy world where she struggled with the devil. It had been life enhancing for her to inform us, but she did not want to expose her secret world to others. She decided that getting on with her life was the priority and that she was the one who could make the necessary changes.

Family Boundaries

Secrets become secrets because there is a boundary between the self and others. Families have two distinct features that make their secrets so dangerous.

1. *Family members, other than the parents, didn't choose each other but can't get away from each other, no matter how many miles apart.* Often secrets are based on clearly divergent preferences and choices to which other family members object. For example, a moralistic or opinionated sibling might never be trustworthy but still be privy to your secrets.

2. *Families are bound by primal attachments.* Love is supposed to bridge the space between family members, re-creating the first few months of life when "Mommy and Daddy and I are one." Betrayal of that oneness sends a traumatic ripple throughout an individual's life. When love is an idea that everyone talks about rather than a fact of life in the family, the breakdown of family boundaries is inevitable. Even in the most rigidly controlled families, there will always be a child who points out that the love is not real, and then acts out his or her rage and grief about it.

The re-creation of family boundary violations in later intimate relationships is equally inevitable. Until secret betrayals are exposed and feelings worked through, the family of origin is the template upon which all intimate relationships are constructed. Even when we dedicate ourselves to not being like our parents, we exhibit their behaviors when we are under emotional stress. There is an unconscious compulsion to re-create the childhood hurts until the habits of living are changed.

Anthony, for example, was twenty-eight years old and a rising star in his real estate firm when his secrets crashed in on him. He grew up in a tight-knit Italian community that had not easily tolerated his father's divorce some thirteen years before. His parents' marriage had been tempestuous despite his father being a quiet, private man. Anthony's mother, in contrast, always had something to say, and as far as Anthony was concerned, it was usually a complaint. Anthony's secret was that he had taken on his father's contempt for women in general, and for his mother in particular.

Anthony had two sisters who wanted to be close to him, especially when their father died suddenly of a heart attack. Instead, Anthony withdrew further. He married a non-Italian woman whom everyone thought was just like his mother. Anthony was unaware of this and resented their comments. The marriage was a disaster. His new wife blamed him almost daily for not being considerate or loving enough. Anthony was alone again four months after the marriage. In shock, he accepted his sisters' suggestion that he get into psychotherapy.

Anthony had responded to the crisis by holing up in

the house he had purchased with his inheritance, talking to no one except his sisters. Slowly he faced his shame and began reconnecting with life. He had escaped fulfilling his father's fate only because his wife had not become pregnant. He had a long emotional journey ahead to heal his wounds.

What his sisters could do was limited. Their efforts deepened Anthony's sense of isolation. He withdrew from them because of his contempt for women which he had acquired from his father. However, his sisters' perseverance paid off. They built bridges of love to him. As they grew closer, Anthony and his sisters found the strength to challenge their mother's view of life and eventually help her modify her more difficult behavior. They set clear boundaries around her tendency to complain by jointly refusing to listen to her. Anthony also came to see his sisters as role models for the kind of women with whom he wanted to be involved.

To Whom Does a Family Secret Belong?

In Anthony's case, his secret contempt for women was clearly his own responsibility. He found it life enhancing not to share this with any of his female family members. Anthony did that in therapy and with male friends, many of whom held similar attitudes toward women and who often felt threatened by the emotional changes he was trying to make.

In other situations, a secret can be held for a long time by an older member of the family who has become comfortable keeping it and who insists that others not discuss it. For example, it may be the family rule that nothing unpleasant is discussed. Or that no one is allowed to talk directly to the family member with a problem. Challenging these positions takes courage and patience.

One tool that helps families face long-held secrets is to see the secret as a "family theme." Did all the first-born males in the family kill themselves or were they severely depressed? Are all the second daughters trapped in unhappy love lives? Knowledge, when handled correctly, is power. Adult children who understand and can talk constructively about how their families have suffered can avoid the same traps. Has the secret been dealt with so that it no longer retains its power, or is it still a hot issue? Hot issues need to be discussed. Silence does not make problems go away.

Did the holder of the secret abuse someone sexually or physically? If so, some form of apology usually needs to be made. Or perhaps other people need to be warned so that no one else is hurt. The person holding the secret may have a difficult time understanding the life enhancement of being open with the victim. Third parties are faced with the ethical dilemma of whether or not to step in. This decision should be made carefully. Disclosure should be made with the same care. Blurting out information and then leaving the principals to pick up the pieces creates the worst possible scenario. Planning for disclosure must include a strategy for subsequent steps and how to deal with whatever feelings arise.

TERRY: "Over the years I have developed the reputation in my family as the one who wants to talk everything out. I'm sure I have gone too far with issues in the past, so that my siblings are more cautious with me about sharing things. I now recognize that privacy is a right in families and secrets do belong to individuals. Waiting for the right time to discuss something is an art that I am learning to master through trial and error."

What do you do if you know a secret that a child doesn't know, and the child's parent isn't telling? Whose business is it to tell? As we discussed in chapter 5, a key ingredient to handling secrets is the integrity of the holder of the secret and that person's respect for those affected by the secret. When you are included in a secret, you become a holder and must then look at the Life Enhancement Grid independently and make your own personal choices. We think that a secret always belongs to the person whose secret it is.

Protection Within the Family Boundary

Secrecy within families can be treacherous. Therefore, some boundaries are important to keep. Parents need their privacy, which gives children the message that the parents' relationship is special and different from the relationship parents have with the children. The parents' sex life, for example, is private, a beautiful mystery not to be shared. Financial matters, also, are usually inappropriate to discuss in front of younger family members.

These are secrets that family members can share among themselves but not tell anyone outside the family. Secrets can be kept from the world in a healthy way that does not involve denial and repression. Keeping these secrets within the family can create a positive family boundary and a special sense of identity—for example, "We are the Jones family, and this is what is unique and terrific about us."

Here's another example: Karen's grandmother's treatment for alcoholism was a family secret that didn't have to be shared with the community. Karen and her siblings needed to know, but their friends didn't, so as to protect the grandmother's sense of privacy. Before *Emotional Healing* was published, we gave the manuscript to our parents and asked them if there was anything they would omit. Out of their great generosity they said no, but it was important for us not to reveal secrets without their permission.

What Are the Secrets to Keep Within the Family?

Not all secrets should be told within the family. While many family therapists would disagree with us, we think that the overriding issue is helping adults get on with their lives, not stew in the "family crucible." Children, even adult children, tend to feel responsible for parental unhappiness. Even those who are in absolute rebellion against their parents easily get caught up in the old family drama. A phone call or a holiday appearance can re-open old wounds. This does not heal the wounds; only feeling the pain associated with them does.

Sally, in a recent workshop, told us a family secret that her mother should have kept. When Sally was a child, her grandmother and mother often openly voiced their negative feelings about Sally's father. Sally did not want to hear these comments about her father because it upset her greatly. Sally admired her father and lost her childhood becoming his caretaker.

If her mother and grandmother were of the opinion that her father didn't deserve respect, they should have kept those opinions to themselves. They could have talked to Sally later, when she began to feel the hurtful effects of his alcoholism. As it was, Sally developed little self-esteem from her father's goodwill toward her. Instead, she was trapped in the position of giving him reassurance and feeling ashamed of her mother. She loved her father dearly in spite of his alcoholism. Trapped by the secret knowledge of her mother's contempt for her father, she had no way to deal with the range of feelings her father's erratic behavior elicited in her. Once she had started her healing process, however, she began to see the strengths and limitations of her parents without needing to continue to fix their problems.

The Importance of Timing

Timing is critical in sharing family secrets within a family. Secrets have different intensities for children as they develop. Small children should not be burdened with adult information. Timing is an important part of how you tell a child. Here are some things to remember:

• Be sensitive to how much children can absorb and how to frame information for them. Use childlike language and concepts they can understand. If you are horrified, disgusted, or angry about the behavior you are describing, the child will be affected. Too many family secrets are divulged during drunken confessionals rather than waiting for the right time for the child to have such important information.

• Take your cue from children as to when telling a secret is appropriate. Often they ask questions that will enable you to tell them information they are ready to hear.

• Do not give children information that they are not mature enough to understand. Remember, if you are uncomfortable with an issue, communicate that feeling and use caution. You can scare a child unnecessarily.

• Talk over difficult revelations with another adult. Rehearsals enhance the likelihood that the message you want to send will actually be received.

• Allow children to ask questions. If a parent is emotionally upset when telling a secret, or if the secret is told in a blaming or punitive way, the child won't feel free to bring it up again.

Healing Family Secrets

Family therapy is a powerful tool for healing when family members are willing to be in sacred space together. When children are still young, this is the approach of choice because everyone is included in the process and feelings can be aired within the safety of the therapeutic environment. Family scapegoats can be identified and re-cast. Dysfunctional families usually have substituted the need for power and control for the key features of sacred space—warmth, focused attention, and empathy. Families that learn these latter, healthy tools can use the Life Enhancement Grid to handle their secrets.

When children grow older, family therapy can turn into an attempt to maintain the status quo, as young adult family members move away and have significant new relationships outside the family. These new family members might easily be included, however, in the family's sacred space.

Families with older children who have moved away are often more resistant to reopening the can of worms. The rewards of doing so are great, however. When the unspoken is verbalized, the weight is lifted off everyone's shoulders, even off those who didn't realize they were carrying it—although at this point in the life of the family, many secrets are no longer life enhancing to share. The privacy of newly forming families may take priority over the tug of parents and siblings who wish, for unconscious reasons, to draw a person back into the drama of the family of origin.

This is especially true of the difficult choices that you must make about telling the secret feelings and memories that emerge in your own emotional healing. We have found again and again that talking about how you were hurt to the people who hurt you long ago perpetuates pain and creates new tensions. What is essential is to get on with your life, disentangling yourself from childhood hurts. If parents or siblings are prepared to make amends, they will let you know. Likewise, you can make yourself available without trying to force something to happen.

A useful slogan to remember is "You can't make it work." When parents and children can look into each other's eyes and, with remorse and encouragement, bear witness to each other's pain, there are few more rewarding experiences. For those that have experienced this level of healing, the satisfaction is tremendous. Nevertheless, each person must decide if they have the time and energy for the level of risk taking involved.

Remember, the purpose of examining the family of origin is to free individuals to fulfill themselves as adults, not to redo childhood. It is too late for that. Good psychotherapy releases the human spirit crushed in the past so that people can have fulfilling relationships in the present. Let's look at how this occurred in one family where the children were grown up when the emotional healing began.

When Joe retired after forty years in the steel mills,

he was relieved of the mundane repetitive tasks about which he had complained to his family with "the same regularity that my mother said the rosary," his son Ethan said. Joe's transition to retirement was not going well because he didn't have any idea what to do with his time.

Ethan was forty-two when he reached out to us for help because he saw himself slipping into a "midlife crisis" where "everything I've accomplished seems to be designed to please my father and, simultaneously, to get me away from him as fast as possible." The women in Ethan's life (his wife, his mother, and his sister) were trying to get him to talk to his father, "to have that father-son talk we never had." Ethan wanted help to do this, although he didn't really believe that it was possible because of his assessment of Joe's inability to change. Through many hours of rehearsals, role playing, and intense reexperiencing of feelings stored up in Ethan's heart, he made himself calm and ready to ask Joe to go on a four-day trip to the Civil War memorial in Gettysburg, Pennsylvania, a place his father had wanted to visit for a long time.

The trip was a huge success for both of them, but the "heart-to-heart" conversation did not take place, at least explicitly. They did spend time together, however, and his father listened to Ethan talk without interruption or criticism. He thanked Ethan repeatedly for taking the time to make the trip. Without ever raising the past directly, Ethan felt that the weight of it had been lifted and he could go on to have a warmer relationship with his father in the future.

Family Grieving

The way families grieve usually reflects the way they live. There are so many losses that are part of daily life that pain-avoidant styles become inbedded in simple remarks like "You shouldn't feel that way" or "It's only a game!" While young children are more expressive of feelings than their parents, they are also easily coerced into numbing the profound body feelings that are associated with death and other losses, because no one likes to feel pain. Healthy parents know, however, that the only constructive way out of pain is through it.

TERRY: "I remember at my father's wake, my sister and I were visibly grief-stricken. It seemed so untimely. He had been sober for two years but still died of cirrhosis. All of his children had had major successes in recent months and we felt like we had turned the corner on our self-destructiveness. It just made no sense to us. My uncle took us aside and insisted that we pull ourselves together, arguing that our father was never comfortable with emotions. This was, in fact, true, but the irony of our uncle's comment was not missed. Wasn't our father lying dead because alcohol was easier to handle than feelings? Hadn't his alcoholism taken him deeper into self-destructiveness?

"In the end, we pulled it together to receive the guests 'properly.' Looking back, I am grateful for the incident. In the long run, it deepened my grief work because it starkly pointed out the condition of denial that killed him. The denial of feelings was no longer a secret among my siblings. We could use this event to continue to support each other."

A particularly insidious way of handling grief is to keep secret the flaws of the person who died. This image becomes idealized over time, completely confusing the family. Susan and Tom, for example, were too young to remember their mother when she died in a car crash. All they could recall were stories of how great she was, and the newspaper clippings they read of charity events she'd helped organize. That she ran away from problems and was killed during a flight from her alcoholic husband was conveniently "forgotten." Their father coped by working and drinking harder, and insisting that "life was for the living."

Susan and Tom had not grown up when we met them, even though both were in their late twenties. They each worked at jobs well below their educational potential. They even looked ten years younger than they were, which was surprising since Tom had spent from the age of fourteen to twenty-eight drinking heavily before finding his way to AA. With careful research among surviving relatives, nannies, and housekeepers, they quickly uncovered the true story, for people believed that "it's time they knew."

"Sobering" is the best word for the news they received. They still loved their mother and were angry at their father for his lifetime of abusive behavior. But, a realistic picture emerged of a family in deep trouble, a family that avoided problems by getting away. Mutually supporting one another, Susan and Tom redirected their lives. Rather than following their parents' footsteps, they acknowledged their mother's weaknesses and allowed themselves for the first time to be angry with her. Also, by respectfully challenging each other, they each grew stronger and more self-reliant more quickly than either could have accomplished alone.

Making the World Seem Normal

In our explorations of family secrets, we discover again and again a simple but highly destructive motivation—the vain hope that life will be better if evidence that things are bad is hidden. Anyone who threatens this belief is seen as hostile and must be sanctioned in some way. The next story shows how extreme this impulse can be. Jennifer and Herb, a couple in their midthirties, had one child, Alice, ten, whom Jennifer kept close to her as if Alice were a favorite toy. Herb, a small business owner, often felt excluded but hesitated to speak up for himself for fear of another fight.

Jennifer believed that there should be no secrets between people who loved one another. Conversely, she thought that a couple can have loads of secrets from others, even from extended family members, because they aren't in the "love circle." Inevitably, Jennifer felt betrayed by both Herb and friends. She created angry scenes and reacted harshly to little things, such as innocent lunch meetings between Herb and mutual friends, regardless of gender. She self-righteously believed that she should be "in" on everything. Openness and honesty were her principles. For Herb to think something was too trivial to mention was considered unloving by Jennifer.

Underneath this banner of openness, Jennifer's dark secret was that members of her family of origin lied continuously to each other. Her family's drama was a mystery play in which Jennifer's well-being depended on sorting out lies and ferreting out the "real" story. Jennifer ran into trouble when she told Alice everything, burdening her daughter with confidences as if she were a buddy. It was too much for the child, but Jennifer couldn't stop. She was a crusader, righting the wrongs of the past.

Jennifer found it life enhancing to open up her secrets. She realized that she had projected her own tortured inner child onto others, and had made incorrect life-enhancement calculations about her daughter, her husband, and her friends. Jennifer needed to learn the huge difference between lying and respecting a person's right to privacy. By the time we met this couple, Herb was repeatedly caught concealing things from her. His explanation was simple: "If I tell her I'm having lunch with my brother, she will want a blow-by-blow account of what happened. I want to have a life of my own."

Both Alice and Herb had become burdened by Jennifer's overriding need to know. Alice was overwhelmed by hearing of Jennifer's financial concerns, her jealousies, and all her minor disappointments. Alice just wanted to be a child with her own dreams, hopes, and fears. She did not have Jennifer's history of betrayals. Because of this emotional burden, Alice had started to have trouble in school. Instead of looking at her daughter's anxiety for what it was, Jennifer insisted on placing blame on the school's way of handling things and on Alice's choice of friends. Our task as therapists was to help Herb and Alice work through their anger without blowing the family apart.

The "I" That Remembers

This goal turned out to be almost impossible because Jennifer saw any attempt to let go of control of the family as a threat to her sanity. Ultimately, Herb and Alice realized that they needed to leave Jennifer. Jennifer's rage was inconsolable. She was too angry to sort out her tangle of secrets. Her way had to be the only way.

Even extreme denial can be sustained if a person can enforce his or her perception of reality onto others. For example, a man named John List killed his wife, his mother, and his three children, then disappeared for eighteen years before he was apprehended. When he was found, List had married again. He seemed a normal if not a very assertive fellow. What had happened that had pushed him to murder his whole family, and then what had allowed him to live for eighteen years as if it had never occurred? List lacked human feelings, such as guilt, remorse, and love. He was instead a "human doing." When he had a problem, he did something about it.

List's first wife had tertiary syphilis of the brain, a condition that caused her to be a mentally erratic invalid who was critical and abusive to List. Although seen by many doctors, she kept the secret that her first husband had died of syphilis. She was never properly diagnosed and got sicker and sicker. To please his wife and three children, List spent much more money than he had. When he was faced with losing his job and his house, the idea of putting the family on welfare seemed a fate worse than death. List decided to kill them instead.

How did he reach this conclusion? List was a keeper of secrets. He never said anything to anyone. He never told his family that his job was in jeopardy. He didn't inform them he couldn't afford the mortgage payment. Being religious, he was concerned about his teenage daughter's rebellious behavior, but he didn't discuss this problem either. Neighbors tried to be friendly, but he rebuffed them. Finally, he concluded that killing his family was the only solution. Then, for eighteen years he lived with the secret of the dead, erasing it from his daily consciousness.

List is an extreme example of what can happen when someone refuses to acknowledge or share his secrets. If List had confided in someone, he might have received practical advice about selling his house and buying a more affordable one. People might have told him that adolescents often experiment with their behavior and then return to their parents' values. If his wife had not hidden her first husband's syphilis, she might have been properly diagnosed and treated. This family's problems only got worse because no one was willing to talk about them.

The Limits of Openness

Most people are like John List in one respect: they are trained from childhood to shut off their feelings. Parents do not want to hear their child's every feeling once the child is older than a year or two.

There is a message that parents don't pass on because they themselves don't know it. That message is: there is a choice between feeling something and disclosing it. Breathing into one's body and feeling the emotions that emerge is data collection. Deciding what to do with that information requires the use of the Life Enhancement Grid.

Good Family Secrets

As we saw in Jennifer's case, her compulsion to be open undermined the more important task of being a good mother. Another friend of ours, Sylvia, forty, was still uncomfortable with too much self-disclosure at one time. Her parents, both psychiatrists, were always inquiring about how she felt about everything. She was enraged that they behaved like psychic cannibals. They just wouldn't take "I don't want to talk to you about it" for an answer.

Sylvia's desire to separate her inner life from her parents' curiosity was developmentally appropriate. She was confident of her parents' love, but she also felt capable of managing her own inner life. Perhaps her parents' motivation was unselfish, but she did not experience it that way. Nor did her parents back off when she told them what was life enhancing for her.

This highlights the key point about parental choices regarding self-disclosure: pay attention to a child's feedback. Not only what the child says, but what he or she experiences in other ways. Adoption secrets are an excellent example of this. As we noted before, adopted children should never remember a time when they didn't know they had been adopted. However, the details of the adoption should be revealed gradually, as the child asks questions about it.

There are also secrets of initiation into the world of being a man or being a woman, which are very positive. Going fishing or off to a ball game with dad, without mom, is a bonding experience for a little boy as he moves from the childhood world of his mother into the wider world of males. What is important is that nothing happen during such outings that violates the values he holds with his mother. For example, to take a child to a place where there is drunkenness or foul language would violate this principle. The secrets shared with dad should be positive and exciting, not dangerous. A child wants to be proud of his identification with the same-gender parent, not scared or ashamed.

Likewise, secrets that develop across gender boundaries can be devastating. They activate the terror and sadness inherent in the oedipal drama of loving and competing with your same-gender parent. While some oedipal struggle is inevitable, parents can help their children by leaving them out of the sexual bond, and accepting that this is a mystery a child is not ready to experience.

Janet, for example, was in recovery from overeating and alcoholism. We discovered through historical exploration how her father's willfulness and her mother's pain had inhibited her sexual impulses since childhood. For example, when Janet was a little girl, her parents had a fight. Later, her father invited her to go on a short excursion with him. As they pulled out of the driveway, she could see her mother crying in the backyard. Instantly the thrill of the special trip with dad was transformed into searing guilt for abandoning her mother. Janet was immensely relieved when the car broke down and they had to go home. In this case, the secret—a special relationship with dad—could not feel good because it came at the expense of mom, a clear violation of the other parent. Healthy parents, with real self-esteem, delight in the closeness the other parent shares with a child.

Initiating children into the world of adult gender identity can be a wonderful time. There is great excitement when life-enhancement decisions are made with care, and both parents are working on the same timetable and sharing similar values.

As children grow up, they become fascinated by hiding places and whispering little secrets to others, which helps develop a separate self within the safety of the family system. A positive sense of family secrets and wonder about life is a strong foundation for an adolescent to begin making life-enhancing decisions, which is necessary because with adolescence comes the need to grapple with the mystery of sexuality, the subject of our next chapter.

Family Secrets

	EXPLORATION	CATHARSIS	INDIVIDUATION
1. *In the Soup*	I struggle with my family drama as if I were still a child.	I have emotional outbursts, or I withdraw in silence.	I will be bound by my family's legacy.
2. *Shame Keeps You Silent*	I am loyal to my family. I make rational explanations for my family dysfunction.	I avoid stressful family issues. I fear feeling more pain.	I am alone, alienated from my family. Perhaps someone will understand me.
3. *Telling the Secret*	I listen to others' family stories and discover similarities.	I fear emotional work, but find some relief in telling my story.	I am in a fellowship with others who are on a healing path.
4. *The Telling Works*	I develop personal guidelines for healthy families. I find pleasure in healthy relationships.	I engage in intense emotional work.	I now know the truth, and I don't blame or accuse family members.
5. *Stuck in the Telling*	I aggressively avoid my family. All my friends are from dysfunctional homes.	I work through my fear of criticism and my need to fix my family.	I take responsibility for my part in family relationships. I begin to take risks for my own fulfillment.
6. *Secrets to Tell, Secrets to Keep*	I experiment with new behavior.	I enjoy taking risks. I detach from my family drama by using the Life Enhancement Grid.	I state my truth to people of my choosing.
7. *Freedom*	I enjoy the dance of intimacy and separateness.	I create family whenever appropriate. I am no longer attached to how others will respond.	I have a deep connection with myself. I accept the ebb and flow of connection to others.

8

Sexual Secrets

When we ask our clients to discuss their sexual lives, we usually get two responses. Women make sweeping statements, such as "our lovemaking is wonderful" or "we haven't had sex for a month"; whereas men mumble "fine," for fear of exposing their ignorance, inadequacy, or lack of sexual interest. We push our clients beyond this resistance because honesty is essential for creating a personal sacred space. Most sexual secrets undermine a person's confidence in his or her attractiveness. Secrets become toxic because there has never been a safe place to discuss the personal details of one's sexual experience and fantasies.

Dan and Susan were no exceptions. Dan, age thirty-two, taught English as a second language. Susan, age thirty, was a veterinary assistant. This story describes one of their rare clashes.

Dan and Susan had been married for several years when Susan arrived home early one day to find Dan watching a pornographic video. Shocked, she became angry at this "objectification of women." Over the next several days she became quietly despairing, feeling hurt and ambivalent. Susan wanted to be open-minded, but only felt disgusted. She stopped having sex with Dan.

Dan was stunned by Susan's extreme response. He remembered discussing that he liked erotica. He believed they had agreed that what he did when alone was his private business. Mostly he felt scared. Was this the end of their relationship?

Trying to explore what was going on and how to proceed was a major problem, however, for the subject of sexuality left them at a loss for words. Talking about sex and sexual secrets in the abstract turned out to be far easier than talking about specific concerns.

Susan's opening remark in therapy was, "I don't know what to do, think, or feel. I don't know where the intense reaction came from." She was frightened that her past held some dark secret. Dan acknowledged that his sexual life was not as pleasurable as his sexual fantasies. Specifically, he wished Susan was the responsive and sexually assertive woman of their courtship.

As these shy, young people reflected on their feelings, they found themselves returning to painful childhood memories. Susan was a sexually responsive teenager, but she had labeled her feelings as "sluttish" and shameful. Dan recalled daunting inhibitions that made him fear being sexually vulnerable. Guided by us, they felt the pain of their parents' rejection of their sexuality—making fun of their teenage "heartaches" and trying to crush their efforts at sexual independence. After sharing such revelations, Dan and Susan talked more openly about what they *did* want sexually.

Susan and Dan needed an environment in which to heal, to step away from a seemingly "functional sexual relationship." They were too frightened and too inexperienced to provide that environment for each other. As we shall see in this chapter, telling sexual secrets to the wrong people, or telling the wrong secret at the wrong time, creates suffering and alienation. In addition, sexual secrets should be shared in ways that maintain privacy and a sense of wonder about the great mystery of human sexuality.

What Is a Sexual Secret?

Most people are haunted by sexual injuries that they have rarely, if ever, discussed. Painful sexual secrets involve abuse, degradation, or being taken advantage of by someone. Many of us are also frightened about what excites us; others of us fear that we are inadequate lovers. These secrets take away the fundamental basis of a healthy relationship—the pleasure of another person's company. People with unresolved secrets have inhibitions, shame, or self-destructive behaviors instead.

Resolving sexual secrets is often more difficult when a person is in a relationship because so much is at stake. Many couples don't want to rock the boat for fear of losing the relationship. They keep their secrets rather than risk rejection or, conversely, hurt the other person. In most couples, one partner is perceived as having more "power" than the other, either in terms of control or independence. As two people work out these inequities, they find that one person's sexual pleasure may be another person's pain.

Dan and Susan had different sources of power. Dan brought the majority of the financial resources into the home and was the more passive member of the couple. Susan made most of the daily decisions and controlled their social life. Each felt vulnerable and victimized by the other: Dan, because Susan dominated their personal life; Susan, because Dan made most of the money. Each harbored anger toward the other.

As victims, they each suffered shame for being either submissive or exploited. Self-hatred had grown, making it more and more difficult for them to reach out to others. Victims no longer have a sense of "potency"—that is, their capacity for fulfillment as an adult and a confidence in their attractiveness to others sexually, emotionally, and intellectually. As is often the case, Dan and Susan had no idea how far they had drifted from each other until the crisis opened the conversation between them.

The roots of sexual secrets can be traced back to childhood. Traumas to healthy erotic development, until they are healed, are re-created again and again in adult relationships. As we saw in chapters 6 and 7, parental secrets are passed on to children, both directly and unconsciously. The same is true of sexual secrets. Recently a young woman named Joyce, a successful computer programmer, visited us. Joyce was a compulsive overeater and dieter. She failed to understand that this behavior was connected to her abusive, alcoholic mother. Only when she started making comments that were similar to ones her mother made did Joyce see this. Calling her daughter a "slut" made Joyce realize that she had been deeply hurt by similar comments from her mother.

JOYCE: "I didn't know until much later in life that my mother had been sexually active early. She was so terrified that I would follow her example that she saw sexual innuendo in everything that I did. Her fear and disgust colored the atmosphere in which I matured. I wish she could have understood that I was me, *not* her, and that my feelings and sexual destiny were my own."

Like Joyce, you can understand your own sexual secrets by examining your parents' actions and attitudes. They are in your bones and condition your actions even when you think you know better. To get a perspective on this conditioning, ask yourself the following questions:

1. *To what extent did your parents degrade their and your sexuality?* By "degrade," we mean that by making sex appear dirty, disgusting, or sinful, parents undermined the natural central place sexuality plays in a healthy adult's life.

2. *To what extent did your parents sexualize your natural curiosity about sex and your sensuality as a child?* If children are responded to in a matter-of-fact way and allowed to be playful about their bodies, they will not get drawn into using their bodies to manipulate people later. Children labeled "seductive" quickly learn the rules to a manipulative drama. They are not taught to orient their bodies toward pleasure, but rather to use them as tools of negotiation.

3. *To what extent do you think pleasure and sexuality are frivolous, rather than a serious focus for your life?* When you evaluate your life, do you think career achievements, financial gain, or acts of altruism are a more worthy cause for celebration than the physical pleasures of hugging, touching, or being sexual with another?

4. *To what extent do you see pleasure and sensuality as dangerous or associated with dangerous activities like crime or addiction?* Belief that sex is dirty, along with the reality of sexually transmitted diseases, can lead to a fantasy life that associates pleasure with danger rather than with warmth and loving. When sexual desire is frustrated, fantasies can emerge that involve surmounting this frustration violently through raping or being raped. Of course, this is different from wanting to participate in such crimes. Even victims of childhood sexual violations sometimes find such images exciting in spite of their rage about what happened to them.

5. *Was there a double standard in your family?* Did boys get different messages than girls? Often boys' messages are challenges to perform rather than to feel emotions. "Getting laid" for example, is a boy's image of success. Girls' messages are to look pretty but deny sexual feelings because you may end up acting them out. The double standard has changed for many adolescents but not for their parents. To the extent that messages project hatred onto the gender (e.g., "Boys are animals," "If you act on your sexual feelings, you are a slut"), pain and confusion about sexual secrets will persist.

6. *What was your initiation into adult sexuality, and how were adult pleasures presented to you?* Most people we have talked to had little or no sexual mentoring. They learn, even as adults, through trial and error or by taking in information from the media. It is as if interacting with a mentor were too stimulating. We offer instead the following alternative scenarios of sexual initiation. Let yourself imagine these events happened to you, and then compare them to your own experience.

For women: On the day of your first menstruation, your mother and a few of her close friends took you and your close female friends out to lunch to celebrate your emerging potency. Each woman spoke to you of her knowledge of "woman craft," of her delight in both your sameness with her and your own unique gifts. You are told that you can become any woman you want personally, professionally, spiritually, and sexually. After lunch, you and your mother go to a jewelry store where your father greets you with warmth, affection, and pride. You have your ears pierced, and then your father presents you with a beautiful pair of earrings, wishing you joy and fulfillment in this next phase of your life.

For men: In the summer after your thirteenth birthday, your father and a few of his close friends take you and your close male friends for a week in the wilderness. Your mother was encouraging and supportive but filled with as much wonder and excitement about what would happen as you are. On the trip, the men share their delight at being men, but they also share the hurts, humiliations, and failures that they have faced. The boys work alongside the men to build a sacred circle in the campsite. Questions are asked and answers are given, but you are consistently reminded of the essential mystery of your sexuality. When you return home, the experience of looking into your father's and mother's eyes is never the same. They wish you well, but you no longer belong to them.

We are sure that nothing like these scenarios ever happened to most of you. But can you imagine how differently you would have answered the six questions we posed about sexuality? In spite of this lack of initiation, by carefully examining these questions, your sexual secrets will emerge. The key to sexual happiness is managing the secrets over time. Knowing your secrets gives you the opportunity to maximize your preferences in relationships.

The Secret of Healthy Pleasure: Connoisseurship

In 1958 philosopher of science Michael Polanyi published *Personal Knowledge.* In this book, Polanyi rebuffed "scientific objectivity" as the focus of science and offered instead the image of the "connoisseur"—a person who makes a study of trying to know about life through following his own passion and pleasure.

Transferring this idea to the sexual arena, we view the connoisseur of pleasure as a person passionately interested in the subject matter: the fantasies, the dreams, the impulses, as well as the life history of his or her partner. The connoisseur wants to know about the most intimate and subtle aspects of pleasure, including the romantic, the spiritual, and the erotic. The physical aspects of the sex may be the basis of a spiritual journey. Most contemporary sex therapy focuses mainly on techniques for pleasure and communication. This is the equivalent of repairing a fender on a finely tuned race car: it is important, but not essential.

Opening up secrets does not take the romance or mystery out of sexuality; rather it adds to it because we are no longer afraid to pursue connoisseurship. The connoisseur is not impartial, frivolous, or overindulgent. The most powerful adult bonds are cemented through sexual activity that is fun, and often sacred. The degradation of sexuality masks this beautiful secret. Fear of our sexual secrets makes it hard to achieve self-respect as sexual beings and to bring our sexual impulses naturally into daily life. It is not appropriate to act out all these impulses, but healthy people enjoy secret personal pleasures that take the form of fantasies and flirtations that are not meant to "go anywhere else."

Intimacy can thus be defined by the notion of the connoisseurship of pleasure. David Snarch, a psychologist who wrote *Constructing the Sexual Crucible,* a 1992 groundbreaking book that attempts to outline a synthesis between marital therapy and sex therapy, defines intimacy as knowing and exhibiting a person's inner life to another with the full awareness of what the other person is capable of hearing and seeing. Intimacy, therefore, is not something "we have." I might be very intimate with you, while you are completely incapable of being intimate with me. The healthy person learns to validate his intimacy internally rather than look to others for approval. Intimate lovers are aware of their own secrets and can consistently and predictably report their wishes to another, as well as protect these same loved ones from their darker impulses.

While the discovery of new secrets is a natural part of a connoisseur's life, the intimate relationship is not bound by the dictum that says "If you love me, you'll tell me all." Healthy relationships are not mergers, but are founded on the capacity both to be independent and to cultivate a spirit of harmlessness toward loved ones. Harmlessness, as we defined it earlier, means that I find it distasteful to hurt, convince, or seduce you to do something, even if that action would make me feel good in and of itself. In the twelve-step traditions, people make amends to those they have hurt, unless telling them will cause further harm. This idea is consistent with connoisseurship because connoisseurs are skilled at discerning what will and will not cause harm.

We will show how connoisseurship works using the example of Jane, a thirty-year-old tennis instructor, who, after some years of psychotherapy, was clearly in stage 6 regarding secrets. Her secret to tell, or keep, involved a sexual affair she had had while alone on vacation in Italy. Married for eight years, with a six-year-old daughter, Jane was considering leaving her husband, Jack, after several years of frustration in failing to get him to pay attention to his family obligations instead of his real estate business. He had told her he needed the time to build his business, otherwise, he'd lose opportunities to other members of his company.

When Jane came back to psychotherapy, she had already decided that she needed to tell Jack about the affair and wanted to think through how to do it to improve their marriage. She wanted the affair to be a wake-up call to Jack. When we took her through the Life Enhancement Grid, Jane found that Jack would be hurt, but she wanted him to see that she was serious. Since returning from the trip, she had felt sexually shut down, but Jack hadn't even noticed. Jane believed that she needed to talk openly about her sexual life if she was ever going to be responsive to him again. In rehearsal with us, she imagined that Jack's spirit wakes up when she tells him and that he has to pay attention because others desire her.

Jane was well aware of the risks involved. After carefully planning what she was going to say and when she would say it, Jane decided to talk to Jack in the den when he watched TV, as he did almost every night. It seemed like his turf, and it highlighted the problem. Jack always claimed that he "needed to veg out after work," but he usually did not emerge from the den until well after Jane and their daughter had gone to sleep.

Jane began her confrontation by turning off the television and saying that she wanted to have a serious talk about "saving our marriage." She told Jack she wanted to "be in therapy with [him]" and that she was "ready to separate if he was not willing to." She emphasized that she cared about him, but the vacation had been an opportunity to see that "I could make it on my own." She then told him about her affair with Carlo, a mutual friend who had visited them two years previously. Although shocked and saddened, Jack was able, with Jane's support and perseverance, to discuss his feelings about their marriage late into the night.

Eager to win her back, Jack agreed to go to therapy even though he had previously resisted. He also had new respect for Jane's courage to fight for what she wanted. Jane had been right that Jack would not be harmed but invigorated by her revelation. The hard part for Jack was realizing that he was sacrificing his family for an image of himself as a career success. He found himself in therapy admitting to secrets of insecurity: he was not effectively handling the pressure of real estate sales; he was threatened by the idea of not being a good provider; and he was unsure of himself as a father.

These secrets put a lot of pressure on him because his father had failed in similar ways. Jane, however, kept emphasizing that she was not his mother, who was disappointed in her husband, but Jack's partner, who was disappointed in his lack of attention to her and their daughter. Ultimately, Jack came to see that he had options his father hadn't had. He decided to turn his interest in personal computers into a job. This field did not have the potential for the "big real estate commission," but it gave him more time to be with his family and put him under much less stress.

Jane could not have known that her gamble would be successful. It worked because of careful planning and because she told all the important pieces of the secret, not just the sensational news of sex with Carlo. Carlo's attentiveness was what she had wanted, not Carlo himself.

But What About Love?

Jane and Jack's story illustrates how a destructive relationship can be made healthy. Most people believe the cornerstones of healthy relationships are love and intimacy. In fact, only in completely fractured relationships do people say they don't love each other anymore. Unfortunately, these "notions" of love and intimacy do not have concrete meaning in most relationships challenged by the daily stress over household chores, bills, careers and children.

Individuals in healthy relationships need to have a more physical basis to evaluate and correct the course of their relationships. Love is what a healthy person experiences as a distinct sense of pleasure and well-being in the body. Healthy individuals love life and are eager to return the experience of pleasure to those around them out of genuine gratitude. As Alexander Lowen, M.D., the founder of Bioenergetics Analysis, a form of psychotherapy that carefully integrates bodily functioning with psychological health, puts it: "Pleasure is the creative force in life. It is the only force strong enough to oppose the potential destructiveness of power. Many people believe this role belongs to love. But if love is to be more than a word, it must rest on the experience of pleasure."

Unhealthy people love others who hurt them repeatedly, whom they distrust, and with whom they have no fun. Love, in the unhealthy person, is attachment, loyalty, and dependence. This love is fueled by memories of how it used to be or by hopes about how it could be "if only . . ."

Symptoms Suggestive of Undiscovered Sexual Secrets

As you mature, a distorted capacity for fulfillment and healthy pleasure shows up in symptoms that come in opposite pairs. Adults tend to extreme behavior because such behavior worked in their childhood to protect them from suffering. They usually don't perceive this behavior as being extreme because of the skewed perspective of their childhood. These behaviors include the following:

1. *Inability to masturbate or compulsive masturbation.* Almost everyone has a secret about masturbation because they don't know what the parameters of healthy masturbation are. We believe that when used moderately, masturbation is "making love to yourself"; when overused, it is a debilitating defense against anxiety and pain.

2. *Sexual addiction or loss of interest in sex.* These two imbalances in sexual functioning are very common. They are behavioral symptoms that reflect unresolved anxiety, depression, substance abuse, or overinvolvement with religion.

3. *Body-image issues and eating disorders.* These secrets are increasingly leading people into psychotherapy. When you do not perceive yourself as attractive or, conversely, are obsessed with maintaining an appearance of attraction, little energy is left to think about what pleases you. Exercise, which is pleasurable to healthy people, is thus avoided, causing slower metabolism and other serious health concerns. Conversely, compulsive exercise can mask serious eating disorders "so no one can see how unhappy I am." One of the great ironies of our time is that food secrets have become moralistic, similar to the way sex used to be treated. Now people talk about "sin" foods and have guilt about ingesting too many calories, exploiting the earth, or not caring for their own health. All these concerns are tied into food, while sexual habits go unexamined and undisclosed.

4. *Elaborate fantasy life or inability to fantasize.* A lack of moderation in fantasizing leads to a sense of meaninglessness. A person either feels dead emotionally and therefore unable to fantasize, or so caught up with fantasy that real life is not lived at all. If you don't have a dream about where you are going, it is hard to act creatively. If you dream too much, it is hard to act at all.

Patterns of Sexual Secrets

Once you have identified where your secrets lie, it is then possible to see their patterns. We identify five basic themes which we examine more fully later in this chapter.

1. *Fear of Pleasure:* While few people readily admit to fearing pleasure, almost everyone recognizes the dangers of "living with abandon" or getting "out of control."

2. *Degradation of Pleasure:* Healthy sexual excitement involves a mixture of power, aggression, warmth, and pleasure. In degradation, however, hostility is sexualized. Often inequality exists, with the person in power often being older, richer, or a member of a prestigious group.

3. *Secrets of the Body:* The thoughts we have about our body—its functioning and its appearance—can be a tremendous source of shame, suffering, and self-hate in our image-obsessed, voyeuristic society. Healing requires sharing these secrets. But body talk (e.g., "I'm too fat," "My hair is impossible to control") becomes a problem if it takes over a person's entire inner life; it can also drain energy needed to implement change.

4. *Sexual Infidelity:* Depending on which study you look at, as many as 50 percent of married men and 40 percent of married women have extramarital affairs by age forty. The number of secrets this entails is multiplied geometrically by the little cover-ups that need to be told to maintain the affair.

5. *Hatred of Sexuality:* Perhaps as a response to the above four items, hatred and disgust for the vibrancy of sexuality often takes on a religious fervor. The hatred of sexuality has deeper roots in the fear of losing oneself in the "oceanic feelings" of pleasure and orgasm. These fears are directly linked to the fear of being "out of control" in daily life.

The Sexual Myths We Live By

We encourage couples to ask themselves what are their operating sexual myths. These myths function in concert with the sexual secrets described earlier. Each myth answers the question, What is sex for?

We label the answers *myths* for two reasons. First, answers to this question shape people's sexual choices and behaviors, and, in turn, reflect their character and the way they live their lives. These beliefs, therefore, take on mythic proportions in life, particularly if a person is unaware of them. Second, each myth contains a piece of the whole truth—a lesson that when balanced with other myths yields a richer perception of the sacred mystery of sexuality.

In other words, the purpose of sexuality eludes simplistic definition because each myth is both accurate and limited in some way. Likewise, most people subscribe to each of these myths in different situations. Some of these myths are highlighted here.

Sex Is for Procreation

This classic Judeo-Christian myth is alive and well around the world. It posits the life of the body as alien from the life of the spirit. While many people deny believing in this myth, it often shows up in language that degrades sexual impulses. This myth splits the personality into good and bad—the self-righteous arrogance of the "moral" and the profound guilt of the "fallen." When guilt over a sexual activity becomes overwhelming, individuals shut down their sexual feelings and want to stifle them in others.

The religious myth sees people's role as being good and doing the will of God, as interpreted by themselves and their religious leaders. Sex thus becomes a blessed gift of the divine, but only if used properly—for example, in a monogamous, heterosexual marital bond with a focus on procreation. Deviations from this norm are tests of moral equilibrium.

This myth is a closed system that allows no exit. Tragically, moral systems with little flexibility tend to lead to adversarial relationships with others—the saved versus the unsaved. While most religions have developed systems to deal with divorce or annulment of marriage, this myth forces individuals to defy conventions, usually in secrecy. The problem with this myth is guilt.

Take Sharon and Carl. Sharon was in her thirties and Carl in his forties when they discovered each other while working at a small manufacturing company. Both were married to someone else and were parents of young children. Both Sharon and Carl were also devoutly Christian. They had lost sexual interest in their own partners but could not adequately say why. They had fallen in love over a two-year period. Their secret love grew more difficult as time passed. They didn't even want to go anywhere with their spouses and children for fear of running into each other in a public setting. It had become a situation that had to change. At this point neither their spouses or their children knew, nor had Sharon and Carl acted out their sexual impulses beyond occasional passionate hugs. They each had to find a way through their guilt so that they could stop punishing themselves and each other.

Their dilemma came to a head when, during a fight, Sharon told her husband about Carl. This precipitated the inevitable breakup of two marriages, neither of which had been working well. To progress with their new relationship, however, Carl and Sharon needed to consider the other myths. There were problems in both marriages. Sharon had been resentful of her husband's neurotic overcontrol of the purse strings and impulsive personal spending. Carl had little feeling left for his wife who had withdrawn into a motherhood she didn't even seem to enjoy.

Sex Is for Power

This myth involves pursuing the most beautiful sex object. This is the dominant American sexual myth, although most people deny that they subscribe to it. This myth substitutes power and image for love and closeness, a viewpoint so common that it shows up in almost every television melodrama. When so many actors and actresses are beautiful, it is hard not to believe this myth.

Anyone who has secret fantasies of an enormously attractive partner immediately understands this myth. It is the primary myth in high school dating. The captain of the football team and the sexiest cheerleader are its icons. This myth says that "you will make me feel like a man/woman if I am your lover." Not only that, but also "I feel that way when others envy my conquest." The voyeuristic society thrives on this myth.

More than any other myth, the notion that sex is for power encourages infidelity. Someone else gives me pleasure and fulfillment. Someone else makes me look and feel better. Someone else can take my pain away. The dream usually fades quickly when real life intrudes.

Carl and Sharon had to look carefully at this myth before proceeding with their relationship. Carl was a successful executive and Sharon, thirteen years younger, was a rising star in the company. Both were very attractive physically. Were they playing out an age-old fantasy where the man feels powerful by seducing a younger woman, and the woman is attracted to his power and position?

Sex Is for Romance

This myth is the stuff of Harlequin novels. Sexual feelings emerge without personal initiation or responsibility. Instead, people are swept away by passion. This myth splits sexuality from daily life, and replaces simple pleasures with intrigue and drama. Sex is for romance when we anxiously await the latest piece of juicy gossip in the tabloids or on soap operas. It becomes dangerous when a person wants to be swept away by seducers, or when a person is bored by an individual who does not set off fireworks on the first or second date.

Carl was more of a romantic than Sharon. His first marriage had begun with a whirlwind affair while on vacation. Perhaps this disastrous marriage could have been, and probably should have been, prevented by a longer and more protracted prenuptial relationship. All he remembered was that the shining and inspired woman he married turned into a dependent and unreliable wife once the "honeymoon was over."

Sex Is for Security

This myth attracts those who are preoccupied by their wounded child inside; that is, "You take care of my needs and I'll take care of yours." This myth's dark side is its immaturity and dependency, which inevitably leads to decreased sexual feeling and a shift toward having one's children meet the parent's needs. If you have entered into a sexual relationship to "get the love you want," you are probably operating according to this myth. This myth works fairly well if both partners have the same dependency needs and neither feels overexploited by the other. The myth that sex is for security provides its followers with a special friend who is "there for you" as much, if not more, than for himself or herself.

Sharon and Carl struggled under the yoke of their spouses' security myth. Carl's wife was overwhelmed by the demands of motherhood. Sharon married because she had become pregnant, and appreciated the security provided by a husband and father, but eventually she became enraged by being "taken for granted" and controlled by her husband.

Sex Is for Fun

This is the "live for today, for tomorrow we die" myth, popular among teenagers and freethinkers. The dark side of this Dionysian myth is, of course, addiction and impulsive acting out that hurts oneself and others. While this myth seems shallow, it may be the closest to biological reality. Adults rarely suscribe to the notion that impulsive sex is fulfilling. Certainly in the age of AIDS and other sexually transmitted diseases, these practices have less and less social support. Nevertheless, sexual pleasure exerts a powerful pull. By combining this myth with the idea of the pleasure of another person's company and the spirit of harmlessness, we create a workable erotic myth that does not necessarily require infidelity. Infidelity, perhaps surprisingly, is not the most fun one can have—most affairs we know about involve a few episodes of clumsy sex and a lot of secretive, anguished time on the telephone. We believe that the real riches of erotic discovery are found in long-term monogamous relationships.

Sharon and Carl were not having any fun in their marriages. The "sex is for fun" myth sustained them through the enormous hardship of their divorces and the subsequent blending of their children into a new family.

Gender Differences

Sexual myths have different emphases and meanings between individuals and especially between genders. What is sexual fun for men and for women can diverge dramatically. For example, men commonly need the trappings and titles of power, while women, equally involved in the myth of power, traditionally have been satisfied to simply be associated with powerful men.

Gender barriers are breaking down, and we applaud this change. In our clinical work, however, we find a gender-specific pattern in the sexual secrets. In Deborah Tannen's landmark book, *You Just Don't Understand,* she showed that men use language primarily for problem solving and to establish dominance or submission with others. Women, she found, use language for establishing a feeling of connectedness and belonging, sharing information, and maintaining contact. Sexual secrets follow the same gender pattern. Men's sexual secrets become traumatic because as boys they were afraid to ask for help and assumed they were supposed to "already" know. Women's secrets revolve around being torn from the fabric of their affiliation bonds by a sexual transgression. For both men and women, the problem involves the one secret we talk about so often: shame.

Sharon longed for the deepened dialogue about life

that Carl brought to relationships. Both having had difficult prior marriages, they found ways to talk about what they wanted from each other that would not have been possible without past experience. Carl was often intellectual about things, offering hypothetical situations and solutions about a problematic situation, while Sharon wanted to hear how Carl felt about it instead. Sexually, Carl was more hesitant to talk, wanting things to be "spontaneous." Sharon had long since realized that she would have to speak up about what would please her because it was different for her each time she made love.

Homosexual Secrets

The shame that goes with acting outside culturally accepted norms does not go away within homosexual cultures. In fact, for many individuals it is intensified. Gays and lesbians live with fears of prejudice, and even violence in many communities. This can mean carrying unnecessary guilt and shame well into adulthood. For homosexuals, the Life Enhancement Grid must be skewed in favor of protecting themselves with secrets. As gays and lesbians find each other and form communities, they offer individuals the safety to explore their secrets and heal.

Sam, a thirty-two-year-old Gulf War veteran illustrates the problems of homosexual secrets. Unsure of his own sexuality and sexually frustrated in his marriage, Sam had gone to a local red-light district to witness heterosexual pornography. In a restroom, he was offered fellatio by a man who asked nothing in the way of touching or affection. It awoke in Sam a longing for male companionship that had lain dormant since adolescence.

SAM: "I couldn't believe it, but I found myself accepting his offer. To my horror, I liked the experience. After that, I could not stop thinking about it, sometimes getting sexually aroused, other times just scaring myself. Eventually, I found that I had to go back to the red-light district to get the thoughts to stop for a while. I have no way to understand this stuff. I began to think I was really gay. I don't even talk to these guys. I was terrified but also relieved to have some direction. I had always been passionless with women and therefore ended up feeling sexually inadequate."

Sam was alone with his secret since he was not part of the gay community. Instead, he was falling into a shame-filled pattern of a sexual addiction. Addictions are behaviors that we repeat even though they clearly cause problems in major areas of our lives: our love life, our work, our spirituality.

What Sam was experiencing was primarily a degradation of sexuality, mixed with an overwhelming guilt and a tremendous fear of pleasure. Eventually, he met a man who mentored Sam into the gay community and helped him accept his homosexuality. He could then take greater responsibility for his sexual preference and pursue a healthy sexual bond.

Now that we have looked at the types of sexual secrets, we will explore them in depth by seeing how the sexual myths interact with them.

The Secrets of the Degradation of Pleasure

Degradation—which always involves hostility that is sexualized—is common whenever there is sexual frustration.

The frustrated person imagines that others have power over him. In turn, he fantasizes that he should have such power. This becomes a vicious cycle: the degraded aspires to become a "powerful person," yet is drawn into situations where he is degraded again. Hostility is directed at oneself and at the degrader, but is buried in acting out the degradation. Such hostility cannot be examined until it is exposed.

The myth distorted in degradation is that "sex is for fun." Hostility is justified because a person is doing something that "feels good and no one gets hurt." One-night stands, wife-swapping, sadomasochistic acts, and orgies are all potential scenarios for acts of degradation.

This rationale ignores the long-term effects on the human psyche. What is fun when a person is sexually aroused one night can be painful and self-destructive in the long run. Take Stephanie's experience of being sexually abused from age nine to fourteen by an older cousin. Now forty-five years old, she is married but has chosen not to have children.

STEPHANIE: "I realized when I was fourteen that the sex was wrong, but I really liked my cousin. He was pretty much the only other young person I could do anything with on summer vacations. I sought therapy because the only way I can excite myself is to imagine sex with my cousin again. My husband has no idea about my fantasy and hardly ever initiates sex, either. I feel so much shame about it, but the image of an older boy and a young girl is what works for me."

Stephanie had to understand that reimagining the degradation was a natural way of coping with the childhood betrayal of her innocence. Slowly, as her rage surfaced, Stephanie developed more self-empowering sexual fantasies.

While childhood sexual abuse is the most obvious form of degradation, there are other forms—for example, the desire to be punished or being attracted to people who cannot love you and sometimes don't even like you. Acting out these secrets is the injured person's attempt to cope because these experiences are pleasurable. In degradation, the theme is disempowerment. Often a person regresses to a childlike dependency in the intimate relationship and adopts a paralyzing fear of abandonment.

Seth, for example, is a tall, radiant young man who dated regularly in college. He did not realize he had sexual secrets until he fell head over heels in love with Audrey, whom he met at a computer sales conference. This was a difficult relationship for Seth. He had a history of being with highly critical women who would become angry with him. Seth enjoyed being in a warm relationship but soon found himself looking to apologize in every situation and "making himself wrong before we even talk about it," as Audrey put it. Audrey appreciated his consideration but was puzzled by it. Their relationship developed rapidly. They chose to live together after a four-month courtship. Then Seth's troubles worsened. He started therapy with the following statement:

SETH: "I want so much to please Audrey that I feel like I'm a puppy dog. After we have sex, I find myself crying. It embarrasses me and frightens Audrey. When she tries to be understanding, I think she is smothering me. It feels like a no-win situation. It is new for me to cry at all, let alone openly in front of Audrey, but I am starting to wonder if this relationship is right for me. Perhaps

I need to feel more in control. I am angry that she has so much power over me."

Seth soon discovered that what he loved and missed was his mother's way of caring for him when he was a child. A powerful and assertive woman, his mother had begun to sexualize him when she had been forced to go back to work after an acrimonious divorce. She called Seth her "little man" and looked at him with longing stares that made him uncomfortable. His father, in contrast, had been mean to both Seth and his mother, leaving the young boy little recourse but to try to "make it up" to his mother even though he feared her too. As we uncovered the connection between his feelings and his father's vow not to ever get close to women, Seth found the confidence to seek deeper intimacy with Audrey. He was able to separate Audrey from his mother, and see Audrey as a loving partner.

Let's look at another example concerning degradation in which people become involved in hiding the secret rather than exposing it. Ingrid, thirty-five, with a six-year-old son, came to therapy after recently divorcing an abusive husband. Ingrid had a budding relationship with a man, Lyle, who was separated from his wife. Ingrid was excited and very frightened by the situation.

Sexually, Ingrid was passionate, but she noticed that she felt like a little girl after her lovemaking sessions. She wanted to curl up and be reassured that she was loved. Also, Ingrid realized that she was angry with Lyle because he had a habit of breaking commitments and arriving late for appointments. This made Indrid think that she was a low priority in his life. Lyle told her that his previous wife would never forget a transgression, so Ingrid tried not to keep score. Ingrid believed that if she let her anger show Lyle would leave her forever, but she was losing her ability to control her anger.

Clearly Ingrid needed to learn to speak up for herself. What secret made this so difficult? At first, she didn't have a clue. With time, Ingrid linked her mother's intense rage at men to her own. She also remembered that at age fifteen she often followed her older sister to her waitressing job at a working-class bar. There, Ingrid was exposed to the sexualized interactions between customers and staff. She was terrorized, but no one noticed. One night, Ingrid was brought into the back room to witness "pornographic movies." To this day, she becomes angry when she sees a prostitute or a "men's magazine."

Ingrid had internalized such degradation. She felt if she stood up for herself, the people at the bar would reject her. Maintaining her role as the "innocent young girl," Ingrid never expressed her anger. Her natural capacity for sexual fulfillment was thwarted until she met Lyle. Before this, she equated sex with stooping to the level of "those awful men."

Fear of Pleasure

The fear of pleasure is really a fear of life itself. People who fear pleasure do not believe in a benign universe; instead, they imagine their deepest longings will get them into trouble. This fear originates in early childhood lessons that the art of living is the art of avoiding pain. If you suffer, "it serves you right!" Let's look at a few examples.

Sandy and Andrew are young professionals who had been dating for six months. Sandy hid her affection for Andrew because he had not directly said "I love you."

She believed the myth that "sex is for security" and was preoccupied with "you take care of my needs and I'll take care of yours." Without such guarantees from Andrew, she became disinterested in sex and unwilling to develop a deeper attachment to him. When the myth of security is thoroughly believed, sexual attachment brings along with it the great danger of abandonment. Sandy "gives to get" rather than "takes for herself with gratitude." Inevitably, Sandy became resentful that she was giving so much and not receiving the reward she sought.

Andrew also feared pleasure, believing the myth that "sex is for romance." Fascinated by intrigue and drama, Andrew wanted a woman who overwhelmed him with passion. Andrew needed that "swept away" feeling before he would tell Sandy he loved her. He found himself drawn into flirtations and was envious of other men's lives.

Andrew and Sandy's mutual fear of pleasure caused them to break up. When Sandy demanded expressions of love, Andrew became terrified. He dumped Sandy to search for the passion he missed. While they protected themselves from their greatest fears, Sandy was abandoned and Andrew fruitlessly sought "perfect women." Tragically, unwilling to give up control, neither could love without trying to change the other.

Let's look at why this happens by exploring the experience of another couple. Candace, a successful twenty-seven-year-old sales representative, came to one of our workshops after a year of finding herself characterized by her boyfriend, Gene, as being too sexually preoccupied. Unable to leave any man up to this point in her life, she felt both anger and shame: "Perhaps he was right," she said. Candace, like many young women, dressed "sexy" and appeared to be sexually interested.

Her secret was that she *really was interested*. How can that be such a dangerous secret? The reason is that as much as men deny it and joke about it, a sexually alive woman threatens a man who is unsure of his own masculinity.

Candace had a sexual style in the bedroom that was both romantic and experimental. She believed it was her right to ask for what she liked. She felt guilty when Gene criticized her, but increasingly she also felt angry at being unappreciated. Candace couldn't leave or confront her boyfriend because of the shame derived from the double sexual standard.

With emotional work, Candace went back to Gene with newfound confidence. Gene now faced a mature woman, not a woman with a secret! Candace learned to take pride in her sexual style. It was what made her feel very feminine and very attractive.

Secrets of the Body

The myth that most interacts with body secrets is that "sex is for power." With this myth comes the idea that sexual fulfillment is only for "beautiful people," and you are worthy of it only if you are one of them.

Women have such strongly held body images that eating disorders, body-image disorders, and obsessive behaviors like shopping become ways of coping with the self-hate that this myth creates. Food secrets are deeply tied to sexual secrets. The first way is obvious: what we put in our mouths directly affects our body. The second way is more subtle and insidious: while we can't control our own sexual interests or our partner's, we do decide what we eat. It is the last bastion of control. Food is a way for women to comfort themselves and enjoy autonomy. (Our culture has more relaxed body standards for males, with the exception, perhaps, of baldness.)

Another secret of the body is being unsure, fearful, or even angry when attracted to another person. For example, Edna, a thirty-year-old social worker, came home one night to find a phone message from her coworker Ron. Although forty-five and married, Ron's youthful appearance and easygoing manner made him very attractive to Edna. She had rebuffed Ron's previous sexual approaches, but this night she returned the call.

EDNA: "Ron invited me on an adventure, refusing to explain what he meant. But I knew. The innuendo was obvious and irresistible. Laughingly, I entered into the conversation and it quickly became phone sex. It was thoroughly enjoyable and exciting, more so than it ever could have been if I were face-to-face with him.

"But as soon as the sexual conversation was over, Ron said, 'I'll let you go to sleep' and hung up. I had a very hard time getting to sleep, trying to sort out the mixture of passion, confusion, and shame that I felt."

While this secret phone sex seemed harmless on the surface, Edna had never discussed with Ron what it meant. Edna felt paralyzed because of her sexual attraction to Ron. She didn't want to repeat phone sex, nor was she prepared to be sexually active with a married man. Until she was able to say this to Ron, her pain and fear eroded her confidence to the point that she dreaded their next encounter.

Edna spent time with us practicing confronting Ron. Developing comfort with being sexually excited by another can be achieved through practice and rehearsal in safe environments. After that, a person can go out and face the object of her desire. After an hour of rehearsal in therapy, she went to talk to Ron. Edna stayed calm while she told Ron that she did not want to repeat the experience with him. It was painful for her to reject him, but it was a big step toward developing confidence in herself. Ron's response was to reveal a secret—that he had remained a "frustrated virgin" until he had married at twenty-six. He justified his acting out sexually as "making up for lost opportunities," although he had no intention of disrupting his marriage. Edna felt good about her decision when she heard this and soon found that they were able to have a less sexually charged friendship again.

Secrets of Sexual Infidelity

For his part, Ron had his own sexual secrets. He rationalized his behavior as "benign," unable to see it was an act of infidelity. What did his phone sex mean? Was he unhappy in his marriage? Or was he just interested in outside sexual stimulation? Edna wanted these questions answered. But for Edna to ask them, she had to be willing to provide sacred space for Ron that she was too angry and confused to offer.

Many experts, most notably Frank Pittman, who recently wrote *Private Lies: Infidelity and the Betrayal of Intimacy,* believe infidelities must be revealed if a relationship is to survive. This notion assumes infidelity is the critical secret. Although the promiscuous partner clearly has a serious and potentially addictive problem, sexual infidelity can be a call for help. The spouse usually can't provide such help. The more important questions are: Where has the pleasure in the marriage gone?

What has this wandering member of the family been looking for outside the primary relationship? In Ron's case, a lack of focus on pleasure in the relationship had existed from the beginning. As is common in many instances of infidelity, the myth that "sex is for power" was running Ron's psyche.

When he came to see us on referral from Edna, Ron immediately revealed his shame and confusion about his feelings for Edna. That he had "thoroughly enjoyed" the phone sex complicated matters. The reality was that Ron had to feel the pain of his loneliness. He was lonely in his marriage, he had no deep male friendships, and he missed the "innocent sexual activity" with Edna.

Another case of infidelity based on "sex for power" concerns Peggy, a forty-four-year-old woman with grown children from a marriage that had ended fifteen years before. Peggy was now married to Lou, an investment banker who had repeated flings with younger women. Lou would occasionally confess to Peggy about his affairs. She would bitterly denounce him, but took no other action. Lou had the trappings of power which she was unwilling to give up. Therefore, she competed with these younger women for him. Lou's secret was that as a child his mother had given him tasks well beyond his age, like doing all the family shopping. When he failed to do this well, his mother criticized him endlessly. This abuse led Lou to a style of threatening Peggy and his girlfriends if they even hinted at dissatisfaction with his independence. He was not going to get too close to a woman again. Peggy, unfortunately, had bought into this game a long time ago.

PEGGY: "I clearly had a stake in winning Lou back. He was kind and loving to me, outside of his infidelities.

I could not see throwing the whole relationship away, but I was getting more and more interested in revenge. If he hadn't chosen to go into therapy with me at this time, it was over for me."

In couples sessions it became clear that Lou believed in the myth that "sex is for power." Lou's sexual triumphs made him feel like a man even more than his career success did. But he wanted Peggy because of the stability she provided and the home life they shared.

Lou's real problem was his poor initiation into manhood. Lou had been ignored by a father who had shown little interest in child rearing ever since he missed a chunk of his children's early years during WW II. Lou wanted to be a man but saw men as competitors rather than allies. He had not even played team sports in high school, but rather focused his social activities on intellectual pursuits. At no time in his life could he remember an older man taking him under his wing. It became the job of the women in his life to make Lou feel like a man. Lou was split between the hunger for manhood achieved through sexual conquest and the longing for a stable, loving partner. A male therapist began Lou's initiation into manhood by pointing out how little interest he had in men and male activities. Lou shuddered at the idea of a men's group. He got anxious about just going to lunch with a male colleague if they had no business agenda.

Burdening Peggy with his infidelities was like asking for permission from his mom to do shameful acts. Lou needed to bring his sexual excitement home to Peggy, not his confessions. Unfortunately, only when Peggy initiated divorce proceedings was she able to get Lou's attention. In most cases it would be too late to save a marriage, for the injury to the faithful partner would be beyond repair.

Peggy and Lou, however, shared a strong commitment to working through their pain. Their relationship was sustained by Peggy's courageous acts of seeking divorce and therapy. When agreement exists about what is life enhancing, great emotional pain can be borne.

LOU: "I miss the sexual conquests a great deal, but I know I want more out of life than power and control. When I think of all the hours that I put into my obsessions, I am amazed that I got away with it. I told myself that I deserved all these sexual rewards for my professional success. In fact, I was really creating more and more anxiety for myself, which I would then relieve with more sexual thoughts and actions."

Lou's actions had an underlying meaning which he needed to discover. Most important, Lou had to learn that in healthy relationships, fidelity comes naturally and is not a moral issue.

The Secret Hatred of Sexuality

There is a deep-seated negative attitude toward sexuality that permeates our culture at the same time that sex sells almost every product.

Most people feel guilty about their lusty impulses, even though few admit it. We harbor sexual thoughts and wish they would not bother us. The secret hatred of sexuality is usually inspired by the myth we call "sex is for morality." Those who believe this myth experience paralyzing guilt over what they consider to be deviant sexual impulses. When such impulses emerge, individuals lash out at themselves and at the sources of pleasure.

Susan's case illustrates this point. Twenty-five years old and successful as a cosmetics salesperson, she arrived in therapy angry at men and at herself for "making so many poor choices" in relationships. Susan saw men as animals who had no respect for personal boundaries and "what women like."

Susan's secret emerged quickly. She knew little about spontaneous excitement and even less about healthy male sexuality. Susan's mother had consistently devalued herself as a woman, and Susan's father wanted her to be his little girl—pretty and sweetly seductive, but never mature or self-affirming, let alone self-pleasuring. When men expressed "sexual" rather than "friendly" interest in her, she felt insulted and degraded. Susan idealized men who weren't available or who weren't really interested in her, and rejected those who were. Susan had too much shame to admit to her ignorance about sexual matters and so stumbled around men, consistently getting hurt and then justifying her anger. Susan needed to learn to talk about these matters.

When people like Susan harbor a secret hatred of sexuality, they tend to view the desire for sex, touching, and having fun as selfish. Real loving is thought to involve heroic efforts of understanding and caring. Searching for sexual fulfillment is seen as self-indulgent and disloyal.

Ethan is another example. As a young man he flunked out of college because of alcohol abuse. After he sobered up, he married Sally, the first woman who would move in with him.

ETHAN: "I did not realize how troubled my wife was until our daughter was born. Sally's enthusiastic interest in becoming a mother was quickly replaced by a postpartum depression. She blamed everyone around her for her troubles. I could not direct my attention to anything else but her when I was in the house. I tried so hard, but inevitably I found myself apologizing for being insensitive, believing if only I could be more loving, things would be better."

Ethan felt helpless. He could tell no one his secrets because Sally prohibited it. But he longed to talk to someone who would listen. Ironically, he came to psychotherapy because he felt like a total failure and his wife told him to "go get help."

The myth Ethan learned in therapy is that "sex is for fun." Before this, all he had was "sex for morality" to hold his psyche together in the face of his unbearable situation. The fact was, Ethan was having no fun. He lived out his hatred of pleasure and sexuality under the banner of being "a good man" and having contempt for disloyalty. "Doing the right thing"—staying in a lifeless marriage "for the children"—took priority because the pleasure of closeness was not familiar to him. He had no inner guidance from the soul other than to be a good soldier on a difficult mission.

Until the secrets of this myth were revealed, Ethan could not stand up to his wife, sue for custody of his daughter, and set out on his own. He did not believe in himself enough to do that. He seemed to need his wife as much as she needed him. In sacred space, Ethan exposed his hatred of his own life and began to think about what he wanted.

Using the Life Enhancement Grid to Deal with Sexual Secrets

With this understanding of sexual myths and sexual secrets, the Life Enhancement Grid is a highly effective
means of exploring sexual secrets without wrecking fragile, intimate relationships. Let's look at how it works.

Claudia, twenty-five, is an advertising salesperson
who had been in therapy for anxiety and low self-
esteem. Claudia's problem stemmed from a deep uncertainty about what she wanted out of a close relationship.
She flipped back and forth from independence and anger
to dependence and compliance without knowing how or
why. Claudia feared she was "crazy." The only solace she
found was with women.

Recently Claudia began dating Sam, whom she had
met at an art course. They were immediately attracted to
each other. Unfortunately, her former boyfriend, Ed,
called her up occasionally for a date. Claudia could not
resist his advances because sexual excitement overwhelmed her. Because he believed in the "sex for power"
myth, Ed became even more interested in Claudia once
he knew about Sam. After an afternoon tryst with Ed,
Claudia met Sam at his apartment for dinner. Sam could
immediately tell that something was wrong. Claudia became rigid when he touched her. He pressed for an explanation. Finally, she blurted out her secret love affair.
Claudia begged Sam to help her by allowing her to talk
to him whenever Ed called.

This was a terrible solution. It was not life enhancing
for Sam to know Claudia's secret, let alone feel responsible for her actions. Claudia needed to tell her secret in a
therapeutic environment. She should have said, "Yes,

there is a problem. It has nothing to do with you or with my feelings for you. I have called my therapist and my support group. I will take care of it. Someday I will be able to share it with you."

Claudia's solution forced Sam to either leave a woman he loved or become a caretaker. Even if Sam agreed to deal with Claudia's obsession, their relationship would become a therapeutic one. This would eventually undermine their passion and love because caretaking relationships are dependent ones, whereas healthy erotic relationships are between adults of equal status who choose to "share the pleasure of each other's company."

The ethic that "I must tell you all" is based on the idea that the sexual bond can tolerate all pain. This is simply *not true*. In fact, the healthy sexual bond is precious and needs to be protected with both civility and careful choices about what is life enhancing to share. Long-term monogamous relationships hold the deepest sexual riches, but it is vital that sexual mystery be sustained over the long term for excitement to remain.

As we stated earlier, intimacy is revealing yourself with full awareness of how others will hear you and then dealing openly with their responses. Within sexual secrets, profound opportunities exist to share pleasure and vulnerability with another. But, as we have seen, the darkest aspects of personality (e.g., fear, jealousy, hatred) also emerge. The next chapter offers more direction on how to effectively function with these frightening secrets while not sacrificing the capacity for life enhancement in relationships.

Sexual Secrets—*The Problem of Pleasure*

	EXPLORATION	CATHARSIS	INDIVIDUATION
1. *In the Soup*	Sex is alien from my daily life, whether I am sexually active or abstinent.	I realize that I operate out of some conviction about what "sex is for."	I recognize my isolation in sex, and my inability to communicate about sex.
2. *Shame Keeps You Silent*	I am stuck, aware of my sexual habits that do not work. I want to believe that everything is "fine" about sex.	I recognize my fear of sex and fear of any change in my sexuality. I express anger that "everything" is sexualized.	I recognize that my sexual myths are questionable, and begin to ask for information.
3. *Telling the Secret*	I experiment with new sexual myths, openness, and curiosity.	I use abstinence to get clear about my own preferences. My sexual injuries are exposed. I pursue intense emotional work.	I find the right variety of sexual myths that work for me. I share my sexual truths with others.
4. *The Telling Works*	I focus on identifying my need for control, and my attitudes, especially my inhibition toward pleasure.	Fear of pleasure and not being in control is recognized. I explore the pain of my sexual injuries.	I experiment with taking responsibility for the various sexual choices I can make.
5. *Stuck in the Telling*	I find myself tyrannized by the sexual values of the groups I belong to, even though I chose them.	I intensively explore my negativity about pleasure accepted. My rage about sex is expressed.	I encourage myself and others to take risks despite the threat of pain. I stop using "shoulds" and instead express preferences.
6. *Secrets to Tell, Secrets to Keep*	I develop a sense of mystery and wonder about the uniqueness of each person's sexuality.	I discover my individuality in sexual union. I keep secrets that embrace sexual excitement, using the Life Enhancement Grid.	I express independence and preferences to those I love. Fidelity is a natural expression rather than a moral imperative.
7. *Freedom*	My sexuality is integrated into all aspects of my life. My potency is not dependent on others' responses to me.	I experience mutual pleasure with others without demands or expectations.	I accept the permanence of change in my sexual life.

9

Lower-Self Secrets

This chapter deals with lower-self secrets. By this we mean the aspects of our personalities that reflect attitudes that are life negating, not life enhancing. Life negation is expressed in three ways: distrust to the point of paranoia, fear and shyness to the point of paralysis; and hatred and prejudice to the point of genocide. While most of us keep these negative aspects hidden, they become obvious, as moralists put it, under temptation.

Life-negating impulses begin when the child is traumatized by parental actions taken against the child's natural selfishness. Every child acts as if he or she is the center of the universe. Some thwarting of these impulses naturally take place. We will all, therefore, have some lower self. The more you know of your lower self, the less it will act upon you and your loved ones. The task of healthy individuals is to face the negativity (some may call it "evil") inside themselves; then, find the meaning in it so that choices can be made for positive reasons rather than out of "fear of getting caught" or some moralistic position that your "reward will be in heaven" or "good things come to good people." In fact, large numbers of "bad guys" die peacefully at an old age.

We believe that evil is not inevitable. Carefully examined in a sacred space, a person's negativity yields feelings of hate (anger), hurt (sadness), and fear. Once expressed, the heart opens and allows for love and healthy body pleasure that is both inspirational and transformative. People who have these experiences will try new ways of life based on pleasure and harmlessness.

In his monumental autobiography, *Report to Greco*, Nikos Kazantzakis points to the name Lucifer as a clue to understanding the perpetuation of the lower self. Lucifer holds the light (Lux) of truth but commits the crime of using it for his own self-aggrandizement, rather than sharing it with others. This is consistent with our views. When you please yourself without considering others, you are not operating from the point of view of healthy pleasure. The Life Enhancement Grid requires consideration of all concerned perspectives.

A powerful view of the dark side was developed by Eva Pierrakos in a series of lectures on the "Pathwork," which she gave intermittently while in trance over a twenty-five-year period. These lectures are a comprehensive and intellectually cohesive body of ideas that suggest life's purpose. In *Fear Not Evil*, the title of a posthumously published book, Pierrakos suggested that we have to learn to harness the energy that drives evil impulses, as well as the energy used to bind our dark thoughts and feelings. Pierrakos's Pathwork lectures divide the lower self into three destructive impulses: pride, self-will, and fear. We add a fourth: domination. This is an expression of the pride and self-will.

Identifying the Lower Self

Pierrakos called it the mask, Jung described it as the persona, and Freud labeled it as a function of the ego. All agree, however, there is a part of the personality designed solely for public display. It hides all awareness of socially unacceptable feelings, attitudes, impulses, or beliefs. Many people believe their entire personality is only a mask, completely losing contact with the impulses and other realities of their lower self. Even when these secrets emerge, they are carefully edited by the ego.

The mask maintains and supports pain-avoidant behavior. As described in *Emotional Healing*, to pursue healthy pleasure and life enhancement, you must feel *all* the feelings: grief, hate, and terror, along with joy, comfort, and spiritual ecstasy. That is why uncovering secrets is so valuable—"burying" requires so much energy that releasing the secrets yields a profound sense of vitality and existential gratitude.

The mask represents the person our parents wanted us to become, though not necessarily what they *said* they wanted. But below the mask are the riches of self-discovery and the capacity for sustained intimacy.

To witness your lower self in action, ask yourself what you would do if you committed an act that no one would ever discover and that would bring no negative consequences. Let yourself go. Entertain revenge. Set aside, if only for a few moments, values about never hurting another person. Wish for punishments you think others deserve.

As you do this exercise, you touch the "pride of the gods," wherein you have the right to decide what is just. You may realize that you want your way. If you do, you are touching your self-will. It follows that you must be secretive about these thoughts because you fear being exposed as bad. This exercise helps you taste the most dangerous drug: having personal power over others. Almost all of us had this fantasy as children because we were so powerless. Domination is a kind of power that is different from having authority and using it for mutual life enhancement. Its goal is the power over others, in and of itself.

Full emotional healing requires that you touch your dark side. The question becomes what do you do once you are aware of it. In this chapter, we examine each of the lower self's four aspects separately.

Pride: The Problem of "Being Special"

Monica, a forty-two-year-old divorced woman who worked as an airline terminal representative, suffered from bulimia when she came to our workshop at Esalen. From the beginning, she was the "problem" participant; the person who asked questions at inappropriate times, the one who interrupted other people's work, the one who told long, rambling stories. Monica's tone of voice was angry and abrasive; every time she spoke she challenged someone in the room. The group quickly became irritated with her. We spent more time interacting with her than anyone else. Monica's pride was not of the inflated self-esteem traditionally associated with the word, but based on the desire to be special by insisting on attention.

In her family, Monica had been considered the problem child. She did not understand why this was, and resented and resisted the label. Underneath her resistance lurked the secret of her lower self—something was wrong with her that caused all the family problems. This belief was so painful that all her energy was used to fight and deny it. Consequently, she blamed other people and stayed angry rather than allow herself to experience how hurt she felt.

As the workshop proceeded, Monica began to drop her angry stance and became more vulnerable. One day she faced her dark secret. Monica told us how she felt about being "wrong" and "bad." Everyone in the room knew this feeling. The group now began to support Monica in her work. She revealed her years of struggling with bulimia and found another in the group who had similar concerns. After that, Monica shared her pain instead of her anger. She began to empathize with other people as they told their own stories. She stopped being the problem and became an appreciated member of the group.

Lower-self secrets are painful and the desire to be special so great that people put all their energy into trying to cover them up. When we believe we are special, we develop secrets of pride and eventually become isolated from others. As she applied her new awareness, Monica began to accept that her life had been hard, and that bulimia had made her special. We asked her to put a message on the refrigerator that said "I'm Not Special," and suggested that she find ways to live as a member of her community rather than as a focus of it.

Responding to Pride

People who are arrogant, arbitrary, and officious usually have similar secrets to Monica's. The attraction of pride is the fantasy that somehow it helps people feel better about themselves. When people lack an inner connection to a higher purpose, having others hold them in awe seems overwhelmingly important.

Having self-esteem is not the same as being prideful.

Pride reflects the desire to separate yourself from the human condition in some special way. Self-esteem means having a positive attitude toward yourself in the face of life's mysteries. It directly involves two personality traits:

• Taking personal responsibility for your successes and failures rather than viewing yourself as lucky or victimized.

• Being a risk-taker who realizes that you are the only one who has to live your life. Some personal risks result in rejections, of course, but people who take risks like themselves better than do those who live more cautiously.

Many secrets get mismanaged because of pride and the fear of humiliation and exposure. A person with pride focuses on image management rather than on being real. If you are preoccupied with image management, compliments are discounted because you know that other people don't really know you anyway. Negative reaction still gets in, however, because it confirms how poorly you manage the image portrayed for the public. Hiding who you really are simply does not work.

Eventually, you discover that trying to be someone else is futile, and that realization leads to healthy withdrawal from the charade. The task then becomes developing a taste for the ordinary rather than the glamorous, the human rather than the stellar. This cannot be done without first discovering the secrets we have about wanting to be special.

TERRY: "I spent my childhood wanting to be the best. An oldest son in a family with a tradition of excelling, I was set up for worshiping the icon of pride. To become a psychotherapist, author, and lecturer is in many ways the fulfillment of this insidious mission to make others proud of me. One of my secrets is that I really do take great pleasure in being respected, admired, and having my measure of fame. But when these activities create conflict in me, such as when I cannot commit energy and time to my stated priorities of marriage and family, I have a problem. It is further aggravated because I am an expert in public while unsure of myself as a father at home. Taking on the challenge of raising children fills me with excitement and deepens my sense of humanity. My sons are great teachers about giving up the secrets of pride."

Secrets of Jealousy

Jacie, an attractive sales representative for an international financial business, had a secret. She had lied to her boyfriend, Fred, about her age, saying that she was forty, not forty-six. Jacie was jealous of Fred looking at other women, and was haunted by his previous twenty-something girlfriends. Jacie panicked when she and Fred were planning a trip out of the country. She feared he might see her passport and discover her true age. She came to therapy because her lie was causing her to wake up in tears in the middle of the night. She didn't know what to do.

Clearly Jacie's secret was making her miserable. Even before the trip, she froze whenever old friends recalled the past, fearing the years she graduated from college and high school would be brought up.

We had Jacie ask herself life-enhancement questions using the body scan to assess her answers. It didn't take long for Jacie to discover that her secret cost her too much, and she decided to tell Fred her real age. Sometimes you can't contain a secret because the dishonesty and lack of integrity around it demands release. That was Jacie's case. But Jacie was still jealous. Made aware of this, Fred learned to be more respectful of Jacie's sexual boundaries and to keep his fantasies to himself. Jacie, for her part, realized her jealousy was a legitimate feeling and that she didn't have to compare herself to anyone.

Envy and Greed

The secrets of envy and greed are often deeply buried because they are sins in all world religions. Yet, all of us have felt envy and greed. In our experience, telling a person that you envy him or her tends to be life enhancing. Often the teller either feels ashamed or misunderstood because the listener responds with a self-deprecating remark, like "It's not that great being me." Ironically, this shames the teller further because he is being told that he is a fool for his envy. The listener must be openhearted for the teller to get the most constructive response, one that is neither arrogant nor negative but respectful and appreciative of the intimacy shared.

A few times we have encountered envy of our professional success. We have found it pointless to explain how hard we have worked, or that the rewards are not as grand as imagined. Instead, we thanked these people for the compliment, and turned the conversation to their aspirations, offering support and encouragement. In fact, we learned this response from our mentors, who take delight in our success.

Talking to someone is essential for secrets of envy and greed to be defused. Expressing them is the first step toward managing them. When you and another know what your wishes are, free-floating envy or greed no longer rumble around in your head, getting attached accidentally to a person ahead of you in the supermarket checkout line or to someone with an attractive new hairstyle. Once envy or greed becomes concrete, you can then focus on setting goals that are inspired by your role models. You can improve your life by planning creatively how to achieve a goal.

Self-Will: The Desire to Have One's Own Way

Few myths die harder than the idea that freedom means you can do whatever you want whenever you want to do it. This definition lacks a spiritual component—that is, that we are part of the fabric of life and our actions affect others.

TERRY: "Some years ago I bought a small lettered sign off a rack in a beachfront trinket shop. It read: 'Do it my way: anyone can do it the right way.' I put it up in my home study to remind myself of the depth of pleasure I used to get from winning arguments, being seen as a dominant male, or knowing the quickest directions from one place to the other. My mask over this sort of behavior was that I really like to be helpful to others, but this became transparent even to me when I came up against others who wanted to be helpful to me. It has become one of the measures of my own maturity when I think about, or better still ask, whether someone actually wants my help before I start giving it. My own breakthrough came when I realized that I enjoyed being close to people more than trying to know what's good for them."

There is a phrase that our friend, psychologist Robert Gass, made into a song, "Not My Will But Thine, Lord."

The will can trick you into almost any action with the promise that it is for the good of the other. For example, in *For Your Own Good,* Swiss psychiatrist Alice Miller showed how some parents rationalized abusive treatment of children. In fact, their actions maintained adult positions of power and crushed the children's spirits. Finding the delicate balance between empowering children through accepting their various impulses and setting safe limits is a major challenge for all healthy parents.

Love with No Self-Restraint

Many of our clients want intense attraction and "fireworks" in their relationships, like they see in the movies. Becky, twenty-eight, was no exception. She and her husband, Harry, thirty-one, had been married for seven years. They had met at a college mixer and immediately fell in love. After a whirlwind courtship, they married. By the time they came to see us, however, the marriage was in trouble. Becky relished coming to couples counseling, having already been in a weekly women's support group and in individual therapy.

At the first session, Harry stated he wasn't sure what he was *allowed* to say and what he should keep private. While we remained silent, Becky said that Harry's remarks showed he did not love her very much. She felt that if Harry had recognized her complaints he would know what he could and could not say.

Becky's statements established that her husband must know what she wanted and then do it for her. She would argue endlessly about the merits of any action, rationalizing her jealousies and preferences on the basis of her love and need for closeness. When we introduced the Life Enhancement Grid, Becky latched on to it as further proof of her love. This made no sense to us at all, but Becky reasoned she always considered what was best for Harry. Showing Becky that this was simply not true was a tall order. She had learned a few psychological concepts from her prior therapy and wielded them like weapons to justify her way of loving.

Harry was an angry, beaten man. His passive stance about therapy aggravated Becky and, in her mind, proved his disloyalty to her. Surprisingly, Harry had a successful retail business, yet he had little self-confidence. He described endless fights with Becky over the smallest things. Harry's success at work was a much valued retreat from Becky's relentless dissatisfactions.

HARRY: "She argues for three hours straight. I give up even when I know I'm right just to keep the peace. The house is a mess, but she won't let me help clean it up. She says it's her territory and she wants me to mind my own business. Even worse, she'll become silent for days if I don't do things her way."

While Harry and Becky's situation is extreme, as long as couples are addicted to intense passion in their personal lives, they will end up raging at each other. What was fascinating about this story was how easily Becky and Harry's relationship was maintained and how hard it was to change. Becky derailed our attempts to focus her and her husband on listening to each other, especially when she felt that her views on love and closeness were challenged. We believed that she had little real love in her. But her views were *real for her,* and had to be respected before any positive change could occur.

In this case, we helped Harry by simply taking an interest in him and allowing him to feel his hurt and exhaustion. Before therapy, Harry attributed all of his pain to a difficult childhood of parental neglect and sibling abuse. Becky supported this. Thinking about his own life required Harry to be courageous, because he *had* been severely hurt in childhood, and because he didn't believe he could be fulfilled in his life. Eventually, he left the marriage.

Becky's willfulness illustrates the danger of being overinvolved in self-help without self-restraint. Too often we've seen people as willful as Becky use what they learned in therapy and workshops as weapons, all in the name of openness, closeness, and love. Self-restraint involves maturity. It means listening to the other side, searching for a relationship's higher purpose, and, above all, realizing that doing it your way does not mean another person has to be defeated. It means letting go of the results after you have formed your opinion and taken whatever action is yours to take.

Responding to the Will of Others

Discerning the truth from other people's willfulness is an art. The more obnoxious the other person, the harder it is realizing that sometimes he or she is right. Only self-restraint allows us the time to separate the wheat from the chaff.

Sometimes, however, authorities are wrong. In the following example, the peer pressure of a group, or "groupthink," as George Orwell put it in *1984,* overwhelmed Karen.

KAREN: "Fifteen years ago I was in a group therapy with two charismatic therapists, a number of friends, and other members. At one point the group leaders urged me to share a sexual secret. I felt uncomfortable that my friends in the group would know this secret. But I trusted these therapists and blurted the secret out, even when I knew I did not want to. I wanted to be approved of more than I wanted my own life enhancement. I did get the approval, but there was no catharsis or personal relief. The group members and leaders were pleased with themselves, but I didn't feel good. It had not been my secret alone. It involved another person that some of the group members knew. Nothing came of it and I was assured of some confidentiality, but it wasn't right for me. My confidence in the group members who were friends was always a bit shaky after that."

Handling Will Constructively

Usually the lower self is brought to our attention by actions we wished we had not committed. When "caught," the tendency is to quickly apologize, and then turn the table on the victim by asking, "Why haven't you forgiven me?" or "Why can't you see how hard I am trying to work on this situation?" Willfulness is that part of the dark side that never wants to give in or to "admit we are powerless," because that is a form of death. However, when a person lets go, not only does the spirit survive, but it gets stronger because of the courage expressed.

Specifically, examples of "letting go" are

- Discharging rage safely into pillows or a bed
- Crying convulsively about defeats that occurred long ago but have not been forgotten by the body
- Reexperiencing the anxiety, fear, and even panic that the ego avoids at all costs
- Allowing the flow of silence in quiet moments, such as during meditation or prayer

Sedrick, forty-five, came to psychotherapy when he recognized he was abusively critical of his girlfriend, Sandy, over the smallest things—buying too much cheese for a party, changing her mind, or messing up the tidy home they shared. Previously, Sedrick would have withdrawn from the relationship, believing that he and the woman were incompatible. But now he was aware that nobody could be compatible with his tendency to rage over small things.

Sedrick admitted that he had become as ruthless toward Sandy as his mother had been to his father, his sister, and him. In fact, he was the only one to attempt an intimate relationship since his parents divorced when he was sixteen. Even after we clearly identified the childhood abuse, Sedrick would rage at Sandy. His struggles with his behavior are reflected in the following remark: "I can't stand being the one who is causing the problems again. I'm making the same comments my mother used to make. She was wrong to berate us. Who cared whether the floor was so clean we could eat off it? That house was not a home for any one of us." He wanted to change, but the process of looking at his behavior was excruciatingly painful.

Lashing out in a therapeutic setting relieved some of the tension at home, but Sedrick was still like a tightly strung guitar. Sandy had difficulty not overreacting. Sedrick had to learn that sexual relationships were not wars and that he did not always have to wear his "armor." Could he take his armor off without feeling overly vulnerable to Sandy? He couldn't seem to bear the humiliation of being powerless over his rages (e.g., "a rageaholic"). His will was dedicated to attributing cause for his rages to whoever was around.

For Sedrick, healing his will required him to surrender to his heart. Then his life-enhancement calculations (e.g., learning to keep his criticisms to himself, learning to share his fears and insecurities rather than his bravado) would be based on caring for himself and Sandy, rather than justifying himself. It was very hard for Sedrick to understand that anyone else's preferences could actually be coming from the heart when he was so cut off from his own.

Fear of Life

Sedrick's real problem was not fear of Sandy's criticism but rather a far more profound terror—a fear of life itself. Operating from his will, he did not trust his warm feelings or anyone else's. When pushed to acknowledge this, he said that he did not "believe that people are essentially or even potentially loving."

Alexander Lowen's masterful book *Fear of Life* shows that the need to control actually reflects the fear of living and dying. When we discuss fear of life as a dark secret, we are not talking about the fear that helps you prepare and do your best. These are healthy experiences. Fear is a by-product of almost any form of excitement, from attraction to hostility, and even confusion. When you find yourself holding your breath, especially when there is nothing really dangerous around, you have begun the journey toward awareness of your secrets associated with fear.

Upon exposure, fear leads to unnecessary secretiveness and deepened humiliation. Without a realistic awareness of how fear affects you, life-enhancement decisions are difficult. Fear blocks you from looking at what terrorizes you.

Most people compulsively avoid their fear. They don't even know that it is ruining their lives. We call this the "whistle a happy tune" technique, based on the Rodgers and Hammerstein song. This is essentially a primitive defense mechanism better known as denial.

Cynicism and skepticism are two other mechanisms often used as masks of fear. Anyone who has attempted to expose real vulnerability in their emotional life has run into these responses. Here is a subtle example of how these attitudes can destroy a person's sense of faith in life.

Nick, thirty-four, a recovering alcoholic with an erratic employment history and a habit of moving every three years from state to state, came to us mystified about his life. Despite his best efforts to make sensible, careful decisions, he kept finding himself in communities where he knew no one, in relationships without love, and in jobs that were boring and unsatisfying. Needless to say, Nick was at the "In the Soup" stage.

Nick was the late-life child of two advanced-stage alcoholics. The secret of Nick's lower self was that he believed that no matter what he did, no plan would turn out as expected and no family problem would ever be solved. Because of this belief, he had long ago stopped consulting his feelings when he considered options for his life. He was tired of the hopelessness that ran his life, but he had no faith that life could be different. Since nothing would work, it hardly mattered which option he chose. Therefore, Nick chose arbitrarily and impulsively, never monitoring outcomes. This was hard for him to admit.

He was always disappointed, and he was in pain, but he was only beginning to feel it because in order to cope he had developed a stoicism toward life. When

Nick began to carefully examine the effects of his secret of hopelessness, he could then defuse that secret instead of continually proving it true. Until he could allow himself to feel how deeply in pain he was, Nick's skepticism kept him from using his intuitive capacities.

In Susan Jeffer's book, *Feel the Fear and Do It Anyway,* she points out a useful way to explore your fears. Once you have identified what causes anxiety or fear, ask yourself the question, What is it that I couldn't handle? Then visualize that thing happening and feel the feelings. As you do, your confidence increases and you have a deeper sense of the reality of the situation. You can still choose not to act. Just because you are afraid does not have to mean anything in and of itself. Courage is taking action with fear in your heart. Fearlessness is not a reflection of courage but of being out of touch with the dangers of a given situation.

Here is an example of how to work with your fear. Marianne, an intense, brooding, twenty-seven-year-old university secretary, saw herself as a loyal and loving friend who was constantly being betrayed. Marianne was in stage 5, "Stuck in the Telling," when we met her. In therapy, however, Marianne found she still had trouble facing both her rage and her fear of her rage. Marianne's stories about the abuse she received from her parents and her siblings were told with a flat voice. Marianne could not express her anger because her mother was dying, her father was grief-stricken, and her siblings were rallying around their mother's deathbed. This had been going on for four years, and "Mom [was] hanging in there." We wondered out loud if this was simply the mother's latest attempt to keep the focus on herself. Marianne agreed.

Marianne's anger showed up in her physical appearance, her demeanor, and her facial expression. She would often project the anger onto her friends, although she was mostly unconscious of her intense anger. Marianne was mystified when her friends became sick of her and pulled away, "victimizing" her again.

We asked Marianne for an example of what it was she felt she could not handle. She chose a recent fight in which she insisted that her friend really didn't want to go to a previously agreed upon restaurant. Marianne was angry about being lied to. Thinking about this story led her to memories of feelings of hurt and rage at her parents' many lies. Marianne had to face the secret of her anger because she spent most of her waking hours telling herself she was a victim, not a victimizer. This incident allowed her to see this aspect in herself.

Marianne needed to express these feelings in their full murderous force within the safety of a sacred space. After that, her fears did not have the same power over her. Eventually, she could handle her anger in social situations. Anger then became something she could be conscious of, and could take specific steps to address. She realized that even if her friend was lying, it was not worth it to fuss over a polite lie.

The fear of opening up the can of worms regarding one's dark side justifies *not* doing it, and fuels cynicism about others on their journey toward emotional healing. Such fear and cynicism reflect a failure during childhood to receive enough support to bear one's feelings. Resolving this kind of childhood trauma is difficult. It takes courage and it takes time.

Iris, fifty-one, is an example of a woman who had tried everything—hypnosis, medication, and psychoanalysis—but nothing helped her nagging fears and frequent panic attacks. An otherwise sensible and successful interior designer, Iris kept her secret well. She would calm herself before venturing out, endlessly rehearsing stressful situations in her mind. Iris would make contingency plans so she had ready-made excuses if she had to cancel an appointment.

IRIS: "When I asked Karen and Terry for help with this in front of a large group, I amazed myself because I had always backed down before. I guess I was pretty desperate and was riding on the excitement of the intense cathartic work we had been doing all day. When they asked me to reenact my mother's craziness, I wanted to rush from the room!"

As her exploratory work continued, we discovered that Iris's mother was emotionally disturbed. Iris took pride in "not letting my mother's behavior get to me." Iris had talked ad nauseum about her mother's illness, but she had never reenacted it. It was the last thing she wanted to do. Iris's secret was that she feared she would have the same breakdowns as her mother. Saying her mother was crazy and *showing herself* that she was also capable of being that crazy woman helped Iris accept the effects without going "crazy."

Fear had become the focus of Iris's life, a refuge as familiar as any home. The tragedy was that Iris was taking herself down the road she most feared. When we asked Iris to embody both the crazy mother and her own craziness, she would writhe on a bed screaming, "You are driving me crazy," letting her eyes get as wild as possible. She had to do it many times, week after week, before this exercise became intensely real for her. Simultaneously, her resistance to fear decreased, much to her surprise. We encouraged her to ask herself the question, What is it that I could not handle? In the beginning, her fears were enormous; but as Iris talked about what she thought she could not handle, her anger at how she was treated as a child would emerge. As she embodied that rage, Iris slowly became stronger. After each time she did the exercise, her muscles became more relaxed and the look on her face warmer and more childlike. It would only last a few minutes, but her body was learning a new way of being without using fear as a coping tool.

This emotional healing may seem simple, but it was not easy. Iris's anger was difficult to bear, and sometimes it exploded at loved ones and friends. But slowly Iris realized she was a person who could handle her fear and her rage. She used a phrase, "My mommy's crazy, I am fine," to see herself through the hard times. She still had to cancel occasional appointments and curl up in bed, but she used that time to have temper tantrums rather than feel sorry for herself. Every time she hit the pillow, she distanced herself from her terror of her own decline into madness.

In *Fear of Life,* Alexander Lowen points out that it is no accident that the word *mad* has a double meaning, one of anger and the other insanity. While rage can lead to unacceptable actions, we have found that the constructive channeling of these feelings into pillows, or even chopping wood, leads to an awakening of the human spirit essential to emotional healing.

When Rage Is Turned on Others

In an age when abuses of power are common, each of us must address the aspects of the human spirit that are characterized by the purposeful drive to have power over others. The extreme psychopath enjoys his success without any concern for his transgressions. To fully explore the dark side, the rest of us must each become aware of how our own desires for power function in daily life.

TERRY: "This section was very uncomfortable for me to write because there is much of this love of power for its own sake in my own character. Finding the balance between empowering my sons and keeping some sense of order and personal safety in their lives does not come naturally to me. I am haunted by Alice Miller's accusations that parental authority is often in service of parental needs for control rather than to foster a child's development. I clearly remember the first time I was aware of my unnecessary use of power in my son's life. My wife, Gale, had just expressed exhaustion, and Evan, then only two years old, was still yelling and racing around our bedroom. I ordered him with a loud voice to stop. Evan looked at me as if I was from another planet. I was immediately devastated. I knew I had just done to him what had been done to me. From his point of view, it was senseless tyranny. From then on, I have tried to consider and even discuss his point of view with him when I exercise my authority.

"This method of seeing the other person's point of view is an application of the Life Enhancement Grid. I must consider what is useful for Evan to hear when he is told to stop. The age of the child must be considered. Would it be useful for Evan to hear that I have a dark side? At young ages the world is thought of in terms of "good" guys and "bad" guys. Therefore, that discussion could be highly premature. But it is definitely life enhancing for me to acknowledge such mistakes as overreacting

to a situation. Healthy homes are honest. I do not need
to be perfect in his eyes."

To hold power over others appropriately requires
self-regulation. People with charismatic power or strong
seductive power do not see others as consenting adults,
but rather as people to manipulate, like sales prospects.
The wreckage that a con man or sexual addict leaves behind is immediately obvious only to the victim, making
education a critical component of treatment of such abusive individuals. Instilling a capacity for guilt in those
who have none is still an extremely difficult problem,
one that sometimes appears to be impossible. We encourage you to keep your secrets from these individuals.

Rodney is a relatively benign example of this. When
we met him, he was an extremely handsome and seductive forty-year-old who loved to travel alone in exotic
places. He usually could find a woman's bed within a
few days. Rodney was a delightful man and would respond to letters and calls from these lovers years after he
had seen them. He did not see any problem with this except when his fiancée felt assaulted by reminders of his
past behavior. It took weeks of Perry Mason–like cross-
examination by us for Rodney to see the wreckage of
broken hearts between the lines of these letters. Rodney
couldn't understand that healthy people fall in love when
they have sex and want to make love again to the same
person in the near future. As obvious as that sounds, it
was just an abstract idea to Rodney, who prided himself
in being kind and considerate even as he admitted to
being a seducer. A seducer, however, wants what he
wants when he wants it. It was a big step for him to respond to the calls and letters with a request for no further

contact. Finally, he had realized that he was harming his fiancée and these other women by his previous actions.

This is the essence of the clinical term *narcissistic character*—the substitution of power for love. Narcissism does not mean that a person likes himself in some special way; rather, it means that he has an image of himself that is more important to him than his real self. This image puts a person in a long-term trance. If this trance works in terms of financial success or other achievements, then others sign on, surrounding the narcissistic person with encouragement and support. The public image of Donald Trump is a classic example of how we all participate together to create an image. He received only a slap on the wrist from the bankers when he began his financial slide because they had so much money invested in him already. The bankers needed his image as much as he does.

Exploring Lower-Self Secrets

At the deepest core of our being, we carry beliefs about ourselves as a result of childhood experiences. The more criticism and injury we received, the more negative our core beliefs. Through therapy we can discover these beliefs because they are the foundation upon which our lives are built. While some, including Scott Peck in his book *People of the Lie,* argue there is a line between mental illness and genuine evil, for us it is merely a matter of degree: love turns to hate if the expression of love is thwarted. Childhood trauma is responsible in part for this, although there are many examples of healthy adult children from abusive homes. Beliefs are shaped not only by the experiences we have, but also by *what* and *how* we are taught. Given current knowledge about emotional healing, pharmacology, and neuroscience, certain individuals are so psychopathic that only incarceration can prevent destructive acting out of the dark side.

Once Barbara Walters interviewed a psychopathic murderer. In her friendly and confiding way, Walters tried to get the man to empathize with the children of the woman he murdered. Characteristically, he threatened to hit Walters and destroy the camera if the interview did not stop. He simply could not feel empathy without his hate exploding out. This is not the case for most of us. In a real sense, these secrets challenge us to find the good in our own evil. If you do not look for it, you will be condemned to have it sneak out in the form of self-righteous pride and willful control of others, especially your children.

The key to the healing process is first discovering your core negative beliefs. Some examples of core beliefs are

- "I have nothing to offer."
- "I am unlovable."
- "Nothing in my life will ever improve."
- "I will always fail."
- "I am a selfish, lazy, mean (etc.) person."
- "I have to control myself or I will be bad."
- "There is no reason or profit in being kind, empathetic, loving (etc.)."

Until such secrets are exposed, therapy won't work. Progress is sabotaged by the deep belief that "I am worthless." Therapeutic environments reawaken the traumas only by addresing them directly, by encouraging empathetic listening to others' painful experiences, and by providing exercises that help the body open up to feelings of childhood hurt and rage. We believe that it is an arrogant, if not silly, perspective of Western psychology that simply talking about your problems to a psychotherapist leads to long-term change in mental status or behavior. Rather, we believe that repeated, dramatic catharsis and a deepened capacity of the body to experience intense feelings (both pleasure and pain) are essential for long-term emotional healing.

Ultimately, work with the dark side and its secrets reflects an ability to feel the pain of one's misdeeds without feeling emotionally destroyed. Intolerance to shame and guilt is a primary reason why individuals hesitate to make the journey to emotional vitality. By contrast, healthy individuals want to, and have the energy to, pursue their own healing and other creative passions. They do so with an awareness of their personal boundaries, and they conduct business with others with an aim toward mutual benefit. To stop the lower self from acting out in these situations, self-awareness is needed because there is a fine line between standing up for oneself and simply wanting one's way. Similarly, there is a fine line between having respect for others and shutting down your own self-assertion out of fear of potential consequences. Having authority becomes an awesome responsibility, not some prize that is given to the biggest, toughest, or the brightest. These latter individuals are often too full of pride to manage power without it feeding their own dark aspects and turning themselves into dominators rather than leaders.

It is useful, instead, to remember the healthy authority of the old shaman chief in the movie *The Emerald Forest*. A pivotal moment in the film was when the American engineer, who searched long and hard to find his son lost in the jungle years before, argues with the chief that he should order the engineer's son to return to the world beyond the jungle. The son had been raised by the tribe for the past ten years and didn't want to leave. The shaman tells the engineer that he is chief only because he leads the tribe where the tribe wants to go, not because he has some divine right. His special ability is to listen deeply to the soul of his people.

This concept leads us to the next chapter. Every one of us fears that we don't have the ability to be assertive and responsible. Without a connection to faith in the human spirit, as described in chapter 10, it is not possible to fully manifest your truth and make accurate life-enhancement choices.

Lower-Self Secrets

	EXPLORATION	CATHARSIS	INDIVIDUATION
1. *In the Soup*	I do hurtful things to others that seem to come out of nowhere.	I want to stop this behavior, but my impulses seem to take over.	I admit that I am responsible for my actions, and ask for help.
2. *Shame Keeps You Silent*	I realize something is inside me, but I have no language for it. I discover the mask that hides my dark side from others.	I witness the exposure of the dark side. I become aware of the depth of the cover-up in all of us.	I develop tolerance of my own shame. I ask for help. I begin admitting to dark motives in my psyche.
3. *Telling the Secret*	I tell of childhood experiences of being suppressed and hated. I become aware of how I hold my breath in fear.	I experience how negative I can be when I let my rage show.	I experience some relief in the company of others who accept me as I am, without judgment.
4. *The Telling Works*	I join communities that have no judgment of the lower self. I admit to having enjoyed having "power over" others.	I continue to express my rage, sometimes leading to convulsive heartbreak. I am more aware of my sadistic impulses.	I can bear my dark side. I begin to believe I can be responsible for my actions at this deeper level.
5. *Stuck in the Telling*	I look for problems in any situation, unable to let things be simple. Instead, I overpsychologize.	I learn to "let go, let God." I let others be themselves, with respect. I know how hard it is to do the work.	I relax into the pleasure principle. I don't try to be more than who I am.
6. *Secrets to Tell, Secrets to Keep*	I discover the value of self-restraint. I explore boundaries in all my relationships, aware of my darker impulses.	I discover pleasure in contact, not competition. I protect others from the raging and hurt "wounded child," using the Life Enhancement Grid.	I find the ability to walk away from impossible situations. I do my part by telling my truth when it will enhance the life of another.
7. *Freedom*	I realize that bad things happen to very nice people for no apparent reason. I no longer look for answers to Why? but ask, How can I help?	"Not my will but thine, Lord!" becomes a spiritual truth rather than a slogan.	I accept that I cannot control life but only participate wholeheartedly in its unfolding.

10

The Secrets of the Higher Self

Over the years we have learned that few things are more satisfying than giving our best. But after childhood abuse, we often see ourselves as selfish, lazy, stubborn, disrespectful, wild, cheap, unhappy, defensive, and, of course, over-emotional. We believe we are "no damn good." What escapes us is the biggest secret of all—what we call the higher self—that we are loving, wonderful, and creative human beings.

This higher self can be seen clearly in the face of death. In Raymond Moody's research on near-death experiences published in *Life After Life*, he discovered that the dying face is an experience of judgment, a sort of St. Peter's gate. The judge is actually the dying person himself, and the criteria for judgment is the extent to which that person has given and received love, and the quality of that love.

KAREN: "As my health has deteriorated over the last

few years with the progression of breast cancer, my priorities have become simpler. A full breath feels like a great treasure. To gaze into loving eyes is a banquet. Making plans for a lunch date gives me something to look forward to with enthusiasm.

"I often feel sad. I have lost so much: my mobility, my work, which I have loved, my expectation of seeing what the future holds for my children. Grieving for these losses has been excruciatingly painful, but it has brought me home to the secrets of this chapter — that I do love and am loved. I am making the most of the life I have left. It's very frightening for me. Even with all the meditation and personal development I have pursued over the past twenty years, nothing has fully prepared me for this challenge."

While Karen's situation was extreme, it illuminates the goal of this chapter: to help you discover the secrets of your own greatness and then use the Life Enhancement Grid to make healthy choices.

KAREN: "It took enormous emotional effort before my higher self became a daily experience. I have been angry at my mother for as long as I can remember. But since I have been ashamed of rage, I have occasionally let it leak out in inappropriate self-destructive and irresponsible ways. As I have accepted my anger as simply another form that my caring takes, I have become powerful. I finally feel free from my own self-criticisms."

When we know our fate, we can choose not to fulfill it. As we explained before, fate does not mean destiny, but rather the conditions under which we were raised, nutured, and sometimes traumatized. Without knowing our fate, we do not know how we are predisposed to act based on our history and its secrets. Knowing our fate leads us to embrace our secrets as opportunities for growth, however painful they may be.

Let's look at an example. Gretchen, fifty, came to our workshop looking for a way out of her loneliness. A department store buyer, she was a kind person with a number of good female friends. She had never married, but had had several long-term relationships that had "withered away." She kept herself busy with hobbies and travel, but that wasn't working as well as it used to in keeping her spirits up.

Gretchen jumped into our emotional exercises. She had temper tantrums. She grieved her loneliness. She soaked up the attention and warmth of others in the workshop. Gretchen used "emotional muscles" that had atrophied from neglect. She seemed to appreciate the focused attention given to her feelings. Then one day, Gretchen stepped through the doorway of self-love. She radiated affection toward the group. She saw us as midwives of her birth into the feeling of oneness with her life.

It was an experience of sacredness for Gretchen. By opening her feelings so intensively, she found the events of her life had a customized quality to them, as if they had been just right for her, even the painful parts. This point of view was only temporary, but it changed her life because it provided Gretchen with a foundation to build on. Abraham Maslow, one of the founders of humanistic psychology, labeled this moment a "peak experience." He suggested that people who have them and pay attention to them live rewarding lives. What Gretchen did was let go within the safety of a sacred space and surrender to her own life. This was impossible when she defended herself against her pain and her own secrets. But when a person has worked through his or her fears, then the deepest truth of all emerges: at the core of life is love and creativity.

A Child's Love Is Pleasure

The human capacity for love is found through pleasure. Pleasure begins when a child looks at his or her mother with delight. The basis for all relationships is affiliative trust—that is, a person's trust in her or his own capacity to create a fulfilling relationship with another person.

The mother and child connection deepens into a physical feeling of excitement when later relationships begin. Healthy individuals learn as infants and children to tolerate greater and greater levels of excitement in the form of anger, sadness, fear, and pleasure without losing contact with what is causing the excitement and, equally important, without feeling compelled to *do* anything. Feeling and action are thus separated, so that tools like the Life Enhancement Grid and the Body Scan can be used to evaluate which actions will work best for an individual.

Frequently, people from unhealthy homes have never learned to focus their lives on fulfillment in their relationships either with others or with themselves. Their pain-avoidant coping styles are self-protective and may work up to a certain point in their lives. However, their capacity for pleasure is limited by the pain-avoidant styles they adopt. They have no idea of what they are missing. When spontaneous joy occurs, they experience embarrassment or shut down completely. They see life in terms of good and evil because the pain-avoidant mechanisms invite short-term, self-serving solutions to any problem.

Individuals who drop their pain-avoidant style, however, naturally fall back on what Freud called the pleasure principle. The pleasure principle was unfortunately perceived by Freud as a danger to society because of its aggressive component. In children, the pleasure impulse is, in fact, highly self-centered and shortsighted. Freud suggested that this drive toward pleasure needed to be subjugated to the authority of the ego and the superego if civilization was to develop. Tragically, this shifts the emphasis away from a child's emotional life and capacity for excitement and body feeling to making sure the child behaves "appropriately." Creativity and liveliness must be crushed, or at least must take second place to parental demands. This results in fear and hatred in the child, not the higher-self secrets the healthy individual searches for—such as mutual satisfaction and win-win situations.

Healthy Aggression

Healthy people are aggressive in a goal-directed manner. Others, whose aggression is inhibited, often perceive healthy people as selfish. Unhealthy aggression develops when a child's aggressive impulses are crushed by violence, when parents withhold love and warmth, or when parents use seduction or other forms of lying to serve their own needs rather than the healthy emotional development of the child.

The word *selfish* illustrates the distinction between healthy and unhealthy aggression. In popular usage, "selfish" refers to an individual out of touch or not interested in others' needs. This individual operates without considering the mutual pleasure available through sharing and cooperation. Healthy children, therefore, are "selfish" until they have arrived developmentally at certain abilities, such as having empathy for others, feeling guilt over causing pain in others, and experiencing a sense of the fairness of life. If this "selfishness" is accepted rather than thwarted, the child will not lose the capacity for healthy aggression. Selfishness is thus essential to the natural development of self. This is the key to understanding higher-self secrets.

Unhealthy aggression emerges when energy is not channeled into the pursuit of harmless pleasure. Emotional healing involves the transformation of this unhealthy aggression so that it becomes part of a meaningful personal history. With each catharsis, a person creates an opportunity to focus her or his aggression toward healthy pleasure in both love and work. For example, consider the following statement: "I am still angry when I think about a childhood memory of my father's abuse, but by working it through I do not immediately experience father looming over me when I get in a conflict with someone. Instead, I can be more present in the here and now." The higher-self secret here is that a person's entire life is essential to how he or she will move forward toward healthy pleasure. The higher self can be aggressive when there is a clear positive purpose and other people are considered. Healthy aggression is often kept secret because of the fear of offending someone or of being punished for being aggressive. For many of our clients, the crushing of aggressive impulses happened so often in childhood that delaying creative energy became permanent.

KAREN: "Years ago during a time of intense emotional pain I was in a workshop with a therapist I greatly re-

spected. She guided me on an inward journey to a territory of my personality where I was full of self-loathing. It
was very painful to look at this part of myself that I
thought was hateful and ugly. After a while it seemed to
disappear and suddenly I was filled with the joy of my
divine nature, which felt to me to be at the core of my
life. I still have the piece of paper on which I wrote afterwards, 'If what is at my center is bright light and not a
can of worms, then I can be happy! My God!'

"Everything changed with the experience of myself
as a good and loving person. This was the secret of my
higher self as I have come to know it. Before this time,
most of my energy in life had been spent trying to deny
the secrets of my lower self, especially that I was the bad
daughter who caused my mother to be angry."

What Karen describes usually occurs during special
moments. It is a direct experience of the divine within. It
is a miracle when such a moment occurs. You can
achieve this by feeling your pain (the fear, the sadness,
the hurt, the anger, and the rage). The ego and the body
resist feeling, but the higher self flows naturally when
such resistance is gone. This is one of the higher-self secrets: you don't have to actively work on making yourself
holy in any way, just focus on being present. However,
you do have to do your emotional healing so that resistance to the flow of energy is diminished. Too often we
see individuals skipping this hard work by focusing on
the higher self as if simply prayer or meditation can free
the spirit. The danger is that, when put under stress, your
negativity often emerges from deep inside you unless it is
directly addressed and worked through. Most people
know how to be spiritual in holy places. It is much

harder to manifest the higher self when adrenaline races through your body.

Hatred in the Name of God

At our workshops some individuals find the idea that love and creativity form the core of human identity too abstract because they grew up in homes where hate, cruelty, and disgust were veiled in words of love. Children, even infants, know and feel the difference. But the development of the ego—the "I" that interacts and the "I" that remembers—requires a child to accept the principle that "Mommy and Daddy know what they are doing."

In this way the ego colludes with the family to suppress the child's natural negative reactions to abuse, using such rationalizations as "It wasn't so bad." Most of us don't remember our early childhood enthrallment with the parents we imagined to be our Goddess and God. Instead, we recall times when our parents were fallible. The time of enthrallment with parents was precious because it was also the time when we were fully connected to our pleasure principle. What later becomes healthy aggression, such as assertiveness, self-affirmation, goal directedness, and perseverance, starts in the form of crying, reaching, and sucking, and the wholehearted assertion of our right to comfort and pleasurable contact. In the early stages of enthrallment, infants create their own universe. In nontraumatic conditions, they use these skills to sustain positive results without hatred or punishment from their parents.

Parents who are deprived of fulfillment in their own lives can't help but respond negatively to the incessant demands of a child. Consciously or unconsciously, they set out to show the child who is boss. Parental unhappiness yields further disappointment and erosion of confidence in the child's capacity for fulfillment.

Harriet, a single, forty-eight-year-old banker living in Europe, is an example of how far this hatred can take one away from pleasure. When Harriet came to one of our workshops several years ago, we quickly realized that her need for attention was enormous. She was very difficult to manage. Painfully, we recognized that she needed radical intervention because her concept of the higher self was so off. Harriet's childhood was filled with physical and mental violence. Her parents had hit their children capriciously and repeatedly. She wanted the workshop to nurture her and make up for the deficiencies of her childhood. She hated anyone who did not respond affectionately to her. Harriet insisted that the workshop members serve as her higher self, all-accepting and loving. She clearly wanted to skip the intense emotional work involved in facing the darkness of her childhood. Focusing Harriet on her rage when she was busy justifying her anger seemed like an endless task. She wanted a respite from her rage when dealing with it was in fact the work that needed to be done if healing was to take place.

Harriet had distanced herself so far from her childhood that she didn't know what she cared about and had no sense of her sexuality. Harriet's secret was a longing to receive love. It was masked by insistent, raging demands for love from workshop participants. As workshop leaders, we found ourselves challenged by our own hostile reactions to Harriet. Was she one of our own parents, or could we trust our impulses to respond with equal aggression, insisting that she stop blaming workshop participants for not giving her what she wanted?

The fear of acting out our own cruelty toward Harriet left us with no ground to stand on, given our inexperience with her level of childhood trauma and her particular way of coping with it. We wanted to be helpful but were afraid of having negative responses to her. In short, our fear caused us to cut ourselves off from our higher selves.

Developing a connection with one's higher self can go wrong in the face of trauma. Harriet wanted comfort and nurturing as a child just as much as anyone, but during childhood she had been met with hatred that was justified by parental power. It was all she knew. The pain inflicted on her was too immediate to be ignored. The pleasure impulses lost their priority. Harriet moved to Europe to get away from the pain, but it was still inside her.

As we shall see in the next two examples as well, Harriet needed to learn that accurately managing the Life Enhancement Grid requires that you not get caught up with trying to control pain. Whatever you are experiencing is important information that needs to be collected rather than denied, so that you can make life-enhancing decisions about secrets. Healthy decisions must be inspired by a sense of having a higher self. Tragically, Harriet was missing this critical piece of self, even though she could talk about it as an abstract idea.

Cynisicm About the Higher Self

Family experience distorts the development of a healthy and spontaneous higher self. The way this happens is illustrated by the story of Tommy, a forty-year-old recovering alcoholic who was active in AA. Although he was sober, he had no social life other than AA. Living in a small, barren apartment, Tommy called his life "okay" because it was so much better than it used to be when he was drinking and unemployed, but his life was devoid of any real meaning or purpose beyond making sure he had "three hot meals and a place to sleep."

Tommy grew up in an Irish Catholic family that centered its activities around the church. Tommy interacted with the same children at church, parochial school, Cub Scouts, and Little League. It was a very tight-knit community, but Tommy never really felt a part of it. Tommy's childhood memories were filled with fear of both the church and his parents. He was hit for the smallest infraction both at school and at home. Tommy didn't believe that "God was Love" as the parish priest emphasized. His experience was that God hated Tommy for his childlike impulses, such as temper tantrums, masturbation, and swearing. His older brother and sister taught him that the task of childhood was to not get caught (e.g., do what you feel like and when you get to confesison, don't tell the priest anything).

He was also confused by the hypocrisy of his parents. Tommy observed that his parents were pious and humble on Sunday morning, but spent the rest of the week acting erratically and attacking their children with transparently self-serving judgments of good and evil. He particularly remembered their insisting that he was committing a mortal sin if he talked back to them and that God would punish him. Only slightly less horrible was the crime of leaving his room in disarray.

By his early twenties, what was left of his sense of humor had turned to cynicism. He noticed hypocrisy in others but rarely dared to confront it. Tommy barely made it through college; he drank heavily and had no social life. He had completely turned his back on the church and hardly grieved when his father died. He did not trust others.

When Tommy finally when to AA, God had long been an instrument of oppression to him. The idea of the higher power seemed irrelevant. He just wanted to stay sober. Only by the repeated insistence of his older brother, who was also in the program, did Tommy think that emotional sobriety meant more than staying sober. Another AA member who was his sponsor pushed Tommy to do his emotional work, which eventually led him to us.

After a while, Tommy learned to cry about his childhood and about the time lost to alcoholism and isolation. He raged at pillows. His heart would occasionally be very open. He learned to let himself be touched by others' pain. After this work, AA became a place for him to celebrate healing and life. He began to have a spiritually inspired feeling about the program that was reflected in the renewal of his life.

As he moved into stage 5, "Stuck in the Telling," Tommy became unwilling to venture outside AA or even let relationships within the program develop into nontherapeutic friendships. He was hoping AA would fill the hole left in his life by having turned his back on his childhood and having buried himself in an alcoholic haze. Unfortunately, it was not working.

We assured Tommy that he would sometimes feel empty because the healing process is like the full wave of a breath: it expands to inspired states in sacred healing environments, but it contracts in daily life where people often treat each other like pawns in a power game. Tommy had often felt like this. Slowly he learned to live with the normal ebb and flow of faith in himself and in life, finding a permanent role for his higher self, even when he felt cynical. He quit his job and spent the summer at a spiritual growth center where he found people committed to celebrating life. While AA will always have a central place in his life, Tommy realized that he also needed friends outside of the program.

Overinvolvement with the Higher Self

Alice is an example of a person *too* involved with the higher self. A forty-year-old mother of two grown children, Alice worked at her own wallpaper-hanging business. She also meditated and practiced yoga regularly. All was not well with her, however. Her marriage was debilitating: she played the self-righteous parent while her husband, Chet, enjoyed the role of the "incorrigible youth." For example, Alice would angrily wait for Chet well after the expected time of a meeting. When finally he would show up, Chet would simply reply that the football game he had been watching on television had not ended on time. And he never understood why she was making such a big deal out of his tardiness. They both secretly wanted a separation, but neither had the courage to make a move. They drifted along until Alice started coming to our workshops.

Working with us, she was able to look at the dark side of her righteous position that "everything should be just the way it is," a perspective she had learned from the Eastern spiritual traditions. Alice's image of the higher self was like a parent, sometimes kind and sometimes stern, but always in charge. Alice lived in fear of her lower self, not making her own choices but rather the choices she thought God wanted her to make; she had a habit of

coming up with "cosmic" rationalizations for life's horrors. For example, Alice was in a rage at Chet most of the
time. This did not fit with the image of herself as a holy
person. Her voice had a brittle quality as she justified a
critical comment directed at Chet with the statement that
she had meditated on it and "felt guided to say it." There
would also be arguments when she made a pious comment about how Chet must have "chosen" his absent but
demanding boss to "work through [his] feelings about
[his] dad."

Alice had been the youngest child by six years in a
family that had ignored its problems which included her
father's depression and the older children's poor academic performance and behavior problems at school.
Alice had learned that "if you haven't something nice to
say, don't say it at all." She buried her rage in a sweet-
ness that was initially endearing but eventually became
tiresome.

As Alice explored the Life Enhancement Grid to decide about telling her husband about her desire for a divorce, her body scan revealed enormous tension that she
had been unable to relieve through meditation and yoga.
As time went on, she found a voice inside her that she
called a "raging bitch." She could see that her important
secret was her hostility, but she would rather break into
tears than feel it. Slowly, Alice learned to tolerate her
anger and channel it into hitting pillows rather than raging at Chet. In fact, she came to acknowledge that she
had been frustrated all her life, always trying to be good
when she really felt angry. Now, memories of her mother
not wanting her began to make sense. Alice's spiritual life
reflected a pseudosophistication that mirrored the strict
demands placed on her as a child. Beneath this construct

was the terror of a 4-year-old who believed that the universe was filled with chaos.

We gave her an exercise to get at this childhood terror of rejection and rage. The exercise was to lie on a bed and yell to her parents, "You are driving me crazy." At first she did this very mechanically, and then, eventually, the frustration and exhaustion of vigorously doing this repetitive exercise served as a bridge to the actual intense immediate feeling of rage and fear of being driven out of her mind.

As she relaxed afterwards, Alice was amazed that the exercise could have worked so powerfully. There was a look in her eyes that was different. For a few minutes, the look was that of a warm and present grown-up. It would then fade, but she learned to bring it back more and more easily. Letting herself go crazy helped her give up the spiritual certainty that had annoyed everyone. It had been a mask that she had used to hide from feelings that she could now bear consciously. She held on to the idea of a higher self as if it were a ledge over an abyss.

As Alice developed her feeling side and faced her hostility, she became stronger and more willing to take risks. Finally, she decided she wanted a separation. She was tired of dealing with Chet. She still loved him but simply didn't like being with him. She was going to live each day for herself, something she had never done. Her children, now in college, recognized the change in their mother and slowly began standing up for themselves in relationships. She was pleased that they seemed to be following her lead. The chain of secrets hiding behind self-rightousness was broken.

Alice did not, however, give up her spiritual connection. She got out of being "stuck in the telling." She made room for the dark side in herself so that she could see it and respond to it appropriately in others. Alice had found a genuine higher self, one that she didn't have to keep talking to everyone else about to reassure herself it was there. This change is reminiscent of the Buddhist parable that the truly spiritual person "chops wood and carries water" rather than recites scripture.

Without spiritual meaning in one's life, feeling becomes chaotic. Alexander Lowen describes this as a lack of "grace" in both body and mental outlook. But you cannot try for grace. It emerges as you expose the negative and painful resistance to life's inimitable unfolding in your relationships.

The Pleasure Principle as the Purpose of Life

Let's recap. The pleasure principle is the purpose of life. Love is the concept the body experiences as pleasure. The body is the instrument through which we experience the purpose of life. The principle of harmlessness operates only when the body is free of the conflicts that develop when an individual handles pain through pain-avoidant styles.

If we are moralistic about pleasure rather than collecting information from the body and its feelings, we don't make life-enhancing decisions inspired by the higher self. Instead, we think and act in "good" or "bad" terms, depending on what we believe about ourselves. With practice, we can make highly intuitive and effective life-enhancing decisions by listening to the purpose of life through the language of the body and its feelings.

Zach's story illustrates this ability. Learning to listen to his own intuition came to Zach, like most of us, the hard way—by feeling and causing pain. We call this learning by doing.

Zach and Ed had been best friends since childhood. Now in their forties, with married children, they rarely got together. But when they did, reconnection was easy. They became sidekicks again, "ready for whatever." Ed was the more adventurous of the two. One evening after work, Zach arrived at Ed's office. Ed told Zach to leave his briefcase and follow him, no questions asked. He then took Zach to an elegant restaurant with a unique feature—the servers were all beautiful naked women.

Zach was shocked. Ed teased his buddy for studying the menu and avoiding eye contact with the women. As Zach relaxed, he eventually had a great time. He left the restaurant with a new sense of delight and amazement at his own sexuality. He also had the satisfaction of sharing the event with his friend, like two boys at a fraternity initiation. But guilt gnawed at him. He was ashamed of his male lust and felt guilty about what he perceived to be the degradation of the women. Zach needed to talk about the experience and determine if he should tell his secret, especially to his wife, Rosie. Zach took a longtime female colleague aside and told her the story. Knowing Zach and his wife, she encouraged Zach to put his guilt aside, and warned him not to tell Rosie or "there will be hell to pay."

Zach didn't listen. He told Rosie in as gentle a way as he could, but she exploded anyway. Rosie realized Zach did not commit adultery, but she felt sexually injured and inadequate, messages Zach never wished to send. The story also evoked in her a rage at the degradation of the women at the restaurant. As a result, Rosie stopped feeling sexual toward Zach. Rosie's reaction left Zach with no way to work out his feelings of guilt at home. So he took them to his men's group. There, Zach received support for hating the "objectifying" aspects of male sexuality passed on to him by generations of sexually inhibited ancestors. These women at the restaurant were playing a role for money, and he realized that this was not the genuine sexuality that he wanted in his marriage.

The more Zach talked about the situation with other men, the less interested he was in repeating the experience. It had become an entertaining memory, titillating but distant. He decided that he was not going to let it become a compulsive way of acting out his frustration that Rosie was not, and probably never would be, the realization of his male fantasy of an "uninhibited" woman. Talking about the event helped him have a clear sense of the difference between fantasy and action. Zach became much more comfortable with the pleasure of his fantasies and brought that ease to his sexual life with Rosie.

Real damage had been done, however. Rosie's rage was so intense that a long time passed before she could bring her own sense of what pleasured her back to the conjugal bed. She insisted that her concerns about the degradation of female sexuality in our culture were valid, but she also knew that Zach was not a man who exploited women. Rosie sustained the pain of an internalized sense of second-class citizenship that all women must come to grips with so long as society maintains a double standard for male and female sexuality. Rosie was angry and needed time to work out her feelings.

Couples therapy helped Rosie and Zach to remember that the healthy reason to be together was the pleasure of each other's company. Their individual sexuality was an enhancement of that, not an opportunity to shame each other. As Rosie worked through her pain, she became more sexually provocative with Zach. They learned to meet each other with pleasure and love. Rosie preferred that Zach never return to the dinner club, but also she saw that what he did with his male friends was not her business so long as he maintained their agreements, one of which was sexual fidelity. Zach learned to keep some secrets from this experience: a deepened love for his own sexuality and a greater acceptance that it differed from that of his wife.

Secrets to Tell, Secrets to Keep

As we have shown, when you tell a secret you are disturbing the universe outside your personal boundary. Having certain secrets defines you as separate and unique; keeping harmful secrets—those that shame and embarrass others or yourself—makes it impossible to have a quiet relationship with your inner self. The dilemma is that while some secrets are gems and add to the mystery of life, others are corrosive and erode our sense of peace. This brings us face-to-face with one simple fact: we choose our own destinies.

Throughout this book we have emphasized the value of being conscious of the choices we make. When people insist that a certain response is "just the way I am," they betray the uniqueness and spontaneity of individual situations. Instead, they should be as alert and attentive as possible to internal and external clues regarding life-enhancing choices.

Complete alertness is impossible; perfection is never the goal. Excitement comes from learning about ourselves and other people through trial and error.

KAREN: "Recently I had the experience of being able to accept the love I have always felt for my mother (now dead nineteen years). I spent the day telling my husband, Rick, all the things that I had really admired about her. I cried about all the years I had raged about her. I saw that she had tried to love me, and that she had done the best she could.

"My reasons for my anger are still there. The bad things did happen, but there is now room to remember the good things as well—how smart my mother was, how lovely and gracious, how hard she tried to make good 'motherly' decisions, and how when she was dying, she knitted Christmas stockings for my children so that they would remember the grandmother they hardly knew."

This awakening in Karen happened at a time determined by her own rhythm, not because she decided intellectually to see her mother in a new light. Higher-self secrets are like that. When you work on childhood trauma and secrets using psychodrama or other forms of reexperiencing the past, you create an opportunity to release the energy tied up in hiding from old pain.

We like to think of this time of working through the stages of each secret as "squeezing the miracle out of each of them." We've found that the later stages of handling secrets yield the higher-self perspective of gratitude for the traumatic experiences because they gave us incentive to grow. They are your secrets now, not problems to fear, and they are your gifts to others when you choose to share them. In addition, self-esteem grows when you consciously take the personal risk of being intimate with a chosen person and telling that person about yourself.

The higher-self perspective is not cosmic but rather more open and childlike. It requires a sense of wonder about what it means to be human and about the mysteries of life. You must cultivate awe for life's secrets. In practical terms, this means treating with reverence your own and others' revelations. This sense of wonder can easily be seen in the eyes of children. Sadly, too often it is absent in the eyes of many adults.

The sense of the sacred and the capacity for awe are trademarks of the human spirit. Finding the reverence for life in other species is always a remarkable event. In *The Tangled Wing: Biological Constraints on the Human Spirit,* Melvin Konner describes wild chimpanzees who gaze with awe at a waterfall. He compares this to the astronauts' expressions when they first viewed the Earth from outer space.

People who have integrity and respect for others also have this sense of wonder about the human condition. Healthy individuals bring this awareness to each day and to each encounter. Their relationships are exciting because they resist categorization and, instead, are based on learning more about other people each day. Without this sense of wonder about the mysteries of life, we fear the secrets inside us and those the future holds for us. With wonder, life's unfolding brings a sense of opportunity. Every crisis upsets the status quo and thus becomes an opportunity. Every trauma, whether new or reexperienced in sacred space, is an opportunity to grow. What the future holds for us still retains a sense of mystery, but we are no longer victims of its secrets. When we realize the tremendous power of a toxic secret, it becomes a discovery that can transform our life.

Summary

This book is dedicated to helping you move our society beyond voyeurism and pseudotherapy to emotional maturity, to a place where emotional healing, along with hope, peacefulness and pleasure, is natural and expected. Here are some lessons from the book.

• Keeping a secret can create a sense of self-esteem and personal power, not only for yourself but also for others who would be burdened by it.
• Sharing secrets at the right time builds intimacy and a sense of belonging.
• Sharing secrets builds a sense of safety when reciprocity of self-disclosure is comfortable, and creates deeper intimacy.
• Using the Life Enhancement Grid is an inexact science. We learn to use it through trial and error and with a sense of wonder about how life unfolds.
• Ultimately, maintaining a sense of the sacred in self-disclosure is the key, not giving in to the voyeuristic impulses of our culture.

As you work with your secrets, you may find yourself looking for the answers to some of life's bigger questions. What is the secret of my life? Its purpose, its meaning? Why am I here? What am I to accomplish? Why did I have the parents I had? Why has my life been so hard? These are questions that occupy a lot of us. For some of us, there may be answers; for others, there is no apparent response. Although there are many things that we can control, there are some things that we cannot. The challenge is to learn to accept—and even enjoy—the mysterious elements of our lives. Sometimes this is very difficult to handle. Why did Terry's baby die in childbirth? Why did Karen get breast cancer? Why did your father hurt you? Why did your husband or wife betray you? Why did Karen die?

Although many of us fashion answers to these questions, the truth is, we don't really know. These are life's secrets. Learning to live with them, and knowing how to choose our response to them, is the route to freedom. Freedom involves creating a relationship with your inner world that enlarges, rather than diminishes, your life. Knowing your relationship to your own secret universe—and how much of that to share and with whom—is a place to start.

We can learn only so much about the higher self through sharing other people's stories. Ultimately, we must make sense of our own lives and secrets. By using the simple tool of the body scan and our capacity to feel, we make transactions with others at our personal boundaries by maximizing life enhancement in its most practical form—the experience of pleasure in the body. This pleasure is simple, personal, and often experienced through exploration of (and with) another. It is also the pleasure of leading our own life independently, inspired by a secret inner world. We allow others to have glimpses of it, but it is very much our own.

Two weeks before she died, Karen expressed the following. They were her final thoughts on the higher self and the importance of a spiritually fulfilled life. To die with such grace must be the most profound pleasure a person can experience.

Karen's Journal
April 3, 1993

So I turn my head and look toward death now.
Feeling my way through the tunnel with the space of
emptiness and quiet.
That shimmering silence that awaits me.

Thoughts clutch at my gown as I make my way down the
stony corridors.
Holding me, pulling me back to concerns I am
finished with.

A breath . . . A pause.
I relax, and then float on toward the opening
awaiting me.
This place of peace resides so deep inside me;
It is one, huge and all encompassing.

In the quiet of my mind I find the greatest Truth,
the great Mother/Father.
This is the Hail Mary, the Rod and Staff of Comfort,
The Kingdom and the Glory.

Yea, though I walk through the valley of death,
I will fear no evil.

This is my direction now; inward to the green pastures,
to the great light of divine love, the deep peace of
All Knowing.

The cares of the world concern me no longer.
I have completed this life. My work is done, my
children grown.

My husband is well on his hero's journey.
I have loved much and well.

I do not have a passion to remain, but a
willingness to go.
My body is tired and my soul longs to fly free to the
shores of no pain.

Those I leave behind, I love.
I hope I will remain in their hearts as they will in mine.

Alex, Meg & Max . . . it was a privilege to be your mother.
And Rick . . . a pleasure to be your wife.
Thank you for taking such good care of me.

Dad . . . Thank you for your love, support, and parenting.
Gay and Alden . . . for being my siblings.
And all of you who have been my friends,
for teaching me about love.

Until we meet again.

Higher-Self Secrets

	EXPLORATION	CATHARSIS	INDIVIDUATION
1. *In the Soup*	Spirituality is alien to my inner life.	I became aware of the value to others of the higher self.	I examine my alienation from the higher self.
2. *Shame Keeps You Silent*	I stay away from spirituality, or express the disdain for the higher self. "Religion is the opiate of the people."	I hear people I admire talk of the higher self. I wish to have greater connection to meaning in my life.	I begin asking for help, and asking myself the deep questions about life's purpose.
3. *Telling the Secret*	I discover in my own psychology the betrayal of love in favor of control and power.	I am involved in intense emotional work focused on power and control.	I am in fellowship with others on the healing path. Celebrative rituals begin to have meaning for me.
4. *The Telling Works*	I find "little miracles" occur as coincidences in my daily life. I learn to surround myself with loving people.	"Letting go, letting God" becomes more than a slogan. I am aware of my fear of "letting go."	Love and creativity begin to take priority over having my own way or prestige.
5. *Stuck in the Telling*	I look for "cosmic" explanations for mishaps, errors, and even horrors.	I finally recognize bargains I make in my head with God, as if life were a game instead of a mystery.	I have tired of talking about the higher power as if it were a person. I take responsibility for my own actions.
6. *Secrets to Tell, Secrets to Keep*	I have a strong sense of wonder about life and my place in it.	I take risks speaking my truth. I use the Life Enhancement Grid.	I accept the consequences of life's unfolding, both the painful and the pleasurable parts.
7. *Freedom*	I let go of desires and preferences.	I find equanimity in the face of tragedy and success. I enjoy the dance of life.	I walk the walk of accepting life. "Not my will but thine, Lord!"

Bibliography

Bednar, Richard L., Wells, M. Gawain, and Peterson, Scott R. *Self-Esteem: Paradoxes and Innovations on Clinical Theory & Practice*. (1989). Washington, DC.: American Psychological Association.

Bradshaw, John. *Bradshaw On: The Family: A Revolutionary Way of Self-Discovery*. (1988). Health Communission.

DeBeauvior, S. *The Pain of Life*. (1962). New York: The World Publishing Company.

Eliot, T. S. *The Family Reunion*. (1969). New York: Harvest-Harcourt Brace.

Gendlin, Eugene. *Focusing*. (1981). New York: Bantam Books.

Hunt, Terry & Karen Paine-Gernée. *Emotional Healing*. (1990). New York: Warner Books.

Jeffers, Susan. *Feel the Fear and Do It Anyway*. (1987). New York: Ballantine Books.

Kazantzakis, Nikos. *Report to Greco*. (1975). Touchstone Books.

Konner, Melvin. *The Tangled Wing: Biological Constraints on the Human Spirit*. (1980). New York: Holt, Rhinehart & Winston.

Lawrence, Amy B. *Secrets and Secrecy in Families*. (1989). Unpublished Doctoral Dissertation.

Lazarus, Arnold A. *Marital Myths: Two Dozen Mistaken Beliefs That Can Ruin A Marriage* (1985). Impact Publishers, California.

Lowen, Alexander. *Fear of Life* (1980). New York: Macmillan.

Lowen, Alexander. "*In Defense of Modesty*" (1980). Unpublished Monograph.

Lowen, Alexander. *The Language of the Body* (1958). New York: Macmillan.

Lowen, Alexander. *Narcissim* (1983). New York: Macmillan.

Miller, Alice. *For Your Own Good: Hidden Cruelty in Child-Rearing and the Roots of Violence* (1990). New York: Farrar, Straus and Giroux.

Moody, Raymond. *Life After Life* (1987). New York: Walker & Co.

Orwell, George. *Nineteen Eighty Four* (1950). New York: NAL-Dutton.

Peck, Scott M. *People of the Lie: The Hope for Healing Human Evil* (1985). New York: Simon & Schuster.

Pierrakos, Eva, and Donovan Thesenza. *Fear No Evil: The Pathwork Method of Transforming The Lower Self* (1992). Madison, VA: Pathwork Press.

Pittman, Frank. *Private Lies: Infidelity and the Betrayal of Intimacy* (1989). New York: W.W. Norton.

Polanyi, Michael. *Personal Knowledge: Towards a Post-Critical Philosophy* (1974). Chicago: University of Chicago Press.

Rich, Adrienne. *On Lies, Secrets and Silence* (1979). New York: W.W. Norton.

Schnarch, David M. *Constructing the Sexual Crucible: An Integration of Sexual and Marital Therapy* (1991). New York: W.W. Norton.

Tannen, Deborah. *You Just Don't Understand: Women and Men in Conversation* (1990). New York: William Morrow.

Welwood, John. *Awakening of the Heart: East West Approaches to Psychotherapy and the Healing Relationship* (1983). Shambhala Publishers.

Index